Linda Hoyt · Kelly Davis · Jane Olson · Kelly Boswell

INDEPENDENT   ONE TO ONE   **K-6** SOLUTIONS SERIES   SMALL GROUP   WHOLE CLASS

Solutions
for Reading
Comprehension

Strategic Interventions for *Striving Learners*

Heinemann • Portsmouth, NH

Heinemann
361 Hanover Street
Portsmouth, NH 03801–3912
www.heinemann.com

Offices and agents throughout the world

The authors and publisher wish to thank those who have generously given permission to reprint borrowed material:

Poem, "Thank You, Teachers," adapted from "Thank You, Teacher" by Shelly Bucci, Newcastle, PA. Used by permission of the author.

Cover from *This Little Chick*. Copyright © 2002 by John Lawrence. Reproduced by permission of the publisher, Candlewick Press, Somerville, MA, on behalf of Walker Books, London.

Library of Congress Cataloging-in-Publication Data
 Solutions for reading comprehension : strategic interventions for striving learners, K–6 / Linda Hoyt . . . [et al.].
  p. cm.
 Includes bibliographical references and index.
 ISBN-13: 978-0-325-02967-2
 ISBN-10: 0-325-02967-9
 1. Reading (Elementary).   2. Reading comprehension.   3. Children—Books and reading.   I. Hoyt, Linda.
 LB1573.S7815 2011
 372.4—dc23   2011016624

Editor: Harvey Daniels
Production editor: Abigail M. Heim
Cover and interior design: Lisa Anne Fowler
Cover photography: David Stirling
Interior photography: Larry Crowley, Bill Miller, and David Stirling
Typesetter: Gina Poirier Graphic Design
Customizable Word forms (on CD): Publishers Design & Production Services
Manufacturing: Steve Bernier

Printed in the United States of America on acid-free paper

15 14 13 12 11 VP 1 2 3 4 5

Thank You, Teachers

Thank you, teachers for looking at ME

For opening doors to all I can be

Thank you, teachers for leading the way

The strategies you teach I can use every day

Thank you, teachers

You notice my strengths

You give me hope and go to great lengths

Thank you, teachers for your motivation

Your time, your energy, and inspiration

Thank you, teachers

I just want to say

These are the words

YOU should hear every day.

Adapted from the work of Shelly Bucci

Table of Contents

Acknowledgments

FROM LINDA: As is true of any professional work, this resource and its final form are the result of many thoughtful, talented individuals. First, we would like to thank the team at Heinemann. Smokey Daniels, our treasured editor, offered clarity of perspective, a broad vision of possibility, and a guiding hand as we worked to craft a format that made this resource as compact, direct, and user-friendly as possible. Abby Heim and Lisa Fowler brought the gift of making our simple pages inviting and formatted in ways that bring classrooms and striving readers into clear focus.

The team of reader/responders was pivotal in helping us identify solutions and tools that most directly support teachers and children whether they reside in regular classrooms or specialty environments, supported by interventionists and specialists. Our most sincere appreciation goes to: Rosemary Lehner, Hudson City Schools, Hudson, Ohio; Debby Tuttle, grade 4 teacher and special educator, Aberdeen, Washington; Sue Harbour, ELL teacher, Jennie Bagnuolo, fifth-grade teacher, Liz Kennedy, middle school teacher, Fort Collins, Colorado; Laura Hook, ESOL Coordinator, Howard County Public School System, Howard County, Maryland; Holly Smith, Literacy Coach/Reading Specialist, Sanibel Island, Florida; Dr. Julie Olson, Director of Elementary Education, ISD 196, Rosemount, Eagan School District, Minnesota; Patty Richards, ELL Lead Teacher ISD 196, Rosemount, Apple Valley, Eagan School District, Minnesota; Kathy Holmdahl Bendlin, Reading Recovery Teacher Leader, ISD 196, Rosemount, Apple Valley, Eagan School District, Minnesota.

FROM KELLY DAVIS: I could not have done this without support from my family, Roger, Kara, and Emily. I also thank my sisters, Mary Ellen and Colleen, for their encouragement and love.

A special thank-you goes to Holly and BK for being my lifelong mentors and "life-support." Thanks to my art-studio friends for being the best cheering squad.

I especially want to thank Pattie Phillips, Leslie Hoeckle, Sharon Shields, Karen Forte, Ami Holdon, Kelly Gilroy, and Sarah Norton, for welcoming solutions I offered to support your students.

Enormous thanks go to Pattie Phillips, Ashley Davis, and Shannon Donnelly for taking photographs to accompany solutions described throughout our book.

Thank you, Linda, for bringing the four of us together as we created this book!

FROM JANE OLSON: I want to thank my family, Keith, Dave, and Dana, for their unwavering support throughout this project; my coauthors Kelly and Kelly, and of course Linda, who brought us all together. My colleagues at ISD 196 provided invaluable feedback and support with photo shoots. To my literacy colleagues from the University of Minnesota, who meet monthly for coffee and conversation—thanks for the Saturdays that you pored over sample chapters.

A special thank-you goes to Dr. Julie Olson, Patty Richards, and Kathy Holmdahl-Bendlin from the Rosemount, Apple Valley, Eagan ISD 196 for reading drafts and providing their expertise in elementary education, English language learners, and Reading Recovery. Their feedback was invaluable as we endeavored to meet the needs of diverse learners.

Finally, I'd like to thank my mom, Carol, for being there, for supporting me, for caring and for all the love. Thanks, Mom.

FROM KELLY BOSWELL: This project would not have been possible without the love and support of my family, Cory, Carson, and Brady. I also thank my sisters, Ginger and Tamara, for not only supporting my work, but for creating classrooms where all children can succeed.

A special thank-you goes to Jerry Bauer, Cherryl Underhill, and Katelin St. Peter-Blair, at Whittier Elementary for supporting the work in this book and opening up your classroom to me.

Thank you, Kelly and Jane, for your trust and your friendship.

Finally, I'd like to thank Linda for believing in me long before I ever believed in myself. I'm honored to call you a mentor and a friend.

Introduction

*I*n classrooms across America, there are increasing numbers of students with specialized learning needs—striving readers who need additional support to reach their academic potential. These learners may be learning English as an additional language, or be identified for special education. They may come from difficult family situations, have suffered from distracted parenting, or have limited academic experience. These learners may have come from homes of poverty or high levels of stress, or simply find learning to read to be challenging. Some may be suffering from past instruction that has focused on a single dimension of the reading process, or a lack of instructional alignment between classroom and intervention settings, leaving them tangled and unable to comprehend.

It is our belief that striving readers are an asset—an opportunity to bring out the best in ourselves and our practice—and that the diversity of need that they bring to our classrooms gives us the opportunity to do our very best work. Striving readers may come to school without the benefit of breakfast or parents who read them to sleep. They may be striving to develop academic language in English, learning to navigate a learning disability, hearing impairment, or physical challenge. But, the bottom line is that we are their teachers and striving readers are our future. It is our job to help them learn to negotiate the texts of their world and become critical, reflective, knowledgeable citizens.

We embrace the fact that striving readers challenge us to see the world through their eyes—to find their strengths as well as their areas of need, or to help them make connections between their home culture and the culture of school. As teachers, we *learn* when individual needs challenge us to adjust our point of view and perspectives. With striving readers as our focus, we grow as educators and learn to operate at the top of our instructional game. And, we applaud the fact that striving readers challenge us to become what educators were always supposed to be: expert professionals who—like a doctor—learn to listen, look, assess, and connect, then take responsive action to create learning environments in which kids get their needs met and striving readers reach their instructional potential.

Commonalities

Although there are resources targeted directly to each of the populations we have listed, we have found from years of classroom experience and careful examination of research that many of the same instructional practices are recommended for each of these groups. It is our goal to showcase those commonalities, to enhance your ability to differentiate within your classroom environments, and to help you carefully match vulnerable learners to the instructional experiences that will help them the most. The goal is to reach for a magic combination of rigor and intimacy—providing face-to-face interactions in which needs of individuals are closely examined, then explicitly linked to instruction.

Our focus is on making your teaching life easier, to help you reach out with great intentionality as you support students who need more help with reading. With this resource in hand, you will have strategic interventions and tools that will help learners reach for deeper levels of understanding and become a force in their own literacy learning.

Strong Evidence Base

Perhaps the best news of all is that a strong research base supports the *solutions* we present, offering assurance that the instructional tools you select from this resource have the greatest potential for success. Be sure to notice the research citations at the beginning of each section, the underlying principles at the end of Parts 1 and 2, and the extensive reference list. These are your guarantee that you are bringing best practices to your striving readers when you match your learners to the supports you find in these pages.

Organization

This isn't the kind of book that you read once and put on the shelf. Instead it is a handbook of possibility that you will want to keep by your side as you confer with and plan instruction for the learners who most need your support. The intent is not for every reader to experience every solution. Rather, like the menu in a restaurant, this is a thoughtfully constructed assortment of instructional possibilities from which you can pick and choose supports that best match the striving readers you serve—across a variety of grouping patterns. The instructional strategies offer variety that will support and extend your instruction with whole-class, small-group, and individual experiences. As you move through the pages, you will quickly see the richness of instruction that is inherent in these highly engaging learning experiences—offering invitations for both teacher and learners to engage in deep thinking and analysis.

Teacher Questions: A Guiding Force

The book is divided into three major sections: Solutions for Navigating Nonfiction, Solutions for Comprehending Fiction, and Solutions for Assessment. Within Parts 1 and 2, solutions for nonfiction and fiction, you will find that the resources are organized around commonly asked questions generated by teachers—like you. To bring you these resources in the most compact and direct format possible, we surveyed teachers around the country, identified the commonalities in their questions, and then selected evidence-based solutions for each question.

Side by Side: Reader Profiles

Following each question there is a Side-by-Side profile of a striving reader. It contains a list of formative assessments and a description of reader development that was gained from the listed assessments, close observation, and artifacts of learning. Following the Side-by-Side profile, you will find a wealth of possible solutions from which you can choose when supporting readers with needs similar to those of the reader in profile.

Assessment Solutions: Informant to Instruction

Part 3, Solutions for Assessment, delivers a wide spectrum of formative assessments that can be easily woven into daily instruction. These assessments are designed to tap into the wide range of understandings and behaviors that effective readers need to become thoughtful and reflective. You will find that these tools fit naturally into small-group instruction, one-to-one conferences, and into the reflective moments that occur when you gather writing samples and artifacts of learning to analyze and better understand the progress of your striving readers.

It is important that you select *assessment solutions* that offer a broad view of each striving reader. The Broad-Spectrum Profile on page 148 is a particularly helpful launch into assessment as it can be used to guide your observations and assist you in examining the wide range of behaviors and understandings that your striving readers need to control.

Please note that, for ease of printing, each of the assessment recording forms is available on the CD-ROM that accompanies this resource. We hope that you take advantage of the electronic versions of the forms to personalize them, adjusting and modifying to meet the needs of your striving readers or your own personal style.

Foundational Understandings: Eight Key Points for Striving Readers

As you consider possibilities for accelerating the achievement of your striving readers, these foundational understandings about instruction in the regular classroom and in intervention-focused environments are essential. A solid foundation for accelerated achievement rests upon the following eight key points.

- Expert Instruction
- Time to Read
- Data-Driven Instruction

A solid foundation

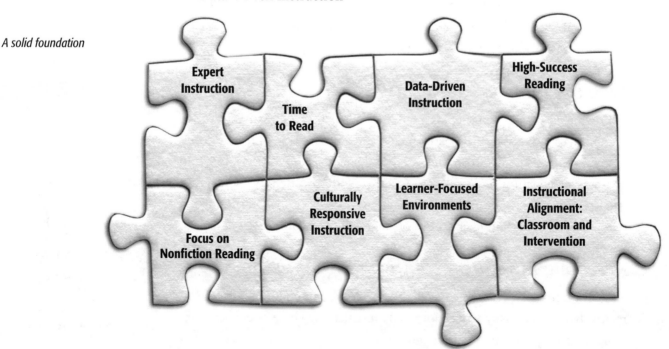

- High-Success Reading
- Focus on Nonfiction Reading
- Culturally Responsive Instruction
- Learner-Focused Environments
- Instructional Alignment: Classroom and Intervention

Expert Instruction: Explicit Modeling, Deep Thinking, and Differentiation

Striving Readers need instruction that is more expert and more intensive than that which is normally provided. Teachers who show outstanding levels of success with striving readers are often heard making statements such as:

> *Watch how I . . . Notice the way that I . . . Look closely as I do this, so you are ready to try this strategy.*

Although this kind of explicit modeling is becoming evident in more and more classrooms around the country, it must be noted that striving readers require more than a single model. To ensure that striving readers fully implement meaning-seeking behaviors, we must ensure that they see these reading behaviors explicitly modeled in multiple situations and multiple texts, and in groups of differing sizes—the smaller the group, the higher the intensity for striving readers. High-quality, explicit modeling along with clear demonstrations of behaviors used by effective readers should be evident in whole-class, small-group, and one-to-one settings (Hoyt 2009; Walker 2005).

For each solution in this resource, we have indicated optimum group sizes with these icons:

Whole Class   One-to-One   Small Group   Partners   Independent

- It is quite clear from long-term outcomes of special education programs, Title I programs, and English language learner initiatives that striving readers experience little benefit from instruction focused primarily on basic skills or from instruction that is separated from that offered in the classroom. What does seem to work is richly-crafted instruction that offers open-ended opportunities for striving readers to make connections, focus on their own questions, and think deeply about content (Cohen and Moffit 2009; Denton, Vaughn, and Fletcher 2003; Freeman and Freeman 2009; Vaughn and Linan-Thompson 2003).

Whole-class setting

Small-group setting

One to one

The regular classroom is where the majority of the learning day is spent, and the first place where schools should begin maximizing learning opportunities for striving readers.

Sketching

Visuals

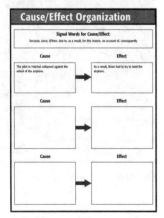

Graphic organizers

- The regular classroom experience is where the majority of the learning day is spent and the first place where schools should begin maximizing learning opportunities for striving readers. Response to Intervention (RTI) suggests that Tier I, the regular classroom, is the cornerstone where high-quality instruction and extensive reading should occur (Brozo 2010). This means that energizing classroom instruction with powerful modeling, deep thinking, and diverse ways to respond to learning is the most important task that schools face when supporting striving readers. Scheduling striving readers for an additional thirty minutes of reading instruction outside of the classroom is not likely to accelerate reading growth unless classroom instruction is improved and enriched (Allington 2010).

- Expert instruction involves differentiation, adjusting scaffolds to meet the needs of striving readers. These scaffolds might include realia and visuals to support concept development and academic language; sketching or dramatizing to consolidate understanding of a concept; adding manipulatives and opportunities for physical interaction to increase engagement; listening to a reading selection on tape before attempting to read it independently; using graphic organizers to visually organize vocabulary and concepts; or time to talk with a partner before attempting to share ideas.

- Expert instruction must be continuously linked to standards so that every instructional minute is treated as a precious pearl (Harwayne 1999). Striving readers are already behind so they do not have time for "filler" activities like acrostics, fill-in-the-blank, or answer the questions at the end of a chapter. They do not have time to fill out study guides that may or may not help to shape the way they approach the next book or learning task. Teachers who provide expert instruction understand that they must teach with a sense of urgency to ensure that striving readers receive the richest, most enticing instruction possible—filling the instructional day with joyous intensity and standards-based learning opportunities that are rich in concept development and language use (Routman 2002). This has special implications for the development of IEPs (Individual Educational Plans) as it is essential that IEPs be standards-based and tightly linked to access of the regular curriculum (Vaughn and Linan-Thompson 2003).

Time to Read: Increase Reading Volume

It is vital that striving readers of all ages have opportunities to build reading stamina by reading more than their higher-achieving peers.

- Striving readers do not need new commercial reading programs—print or electronic. What they need are schoolwide efforts to increase time with accessible texts (Allington 2010). Simply put—striving readers need to read and write . . . a lot.

- Evidence suggests that striving fourth graders who are functioning below grade level expectations may need as many as three to five hours a day of successful reading experience—in books they can read and understand—to have hope of catching up with their more proficient peers. Guthrie and Humenick (2004) and McBride-Chang et al. (1993) suggest that equaling the volume of reading done by better readers will not be sufficient; we need to ensure that striving readers read more than their higher-achieving peers.

- It is of grave concern that many programs designed to provide intervention are not adding additional time with text but rather just replacing a part of the classroom reading instruction with other reading instruction—and too often the adults providing the instruction are less expert than the classroom teacher whose instruction they are replacing (Allington 2009; Short and Fitzsimmons 2007; Vaughn and Linan-Thompson 2003).

- Even worse, observations of reading instruction for striving readers show that these learners are often subjected to lessons in which they are not expected to read very much. Evidence suggests that lessons for striving readers tend to be filled with teacher talk, listening to others read, and lower-level skills such as word study and practice sheets. In contrast, studies of classrooms where striving readers make exceptional progress show that in a thirty-minute lesson, the striving readers were actively engaged as readers for a minimum of twenty minutes with authentic texts and highly engaging topics. In a sixty-minute lesson, those readers spent forty to forty-five minutes reading (Allington 1980; Short and Fitzsimmons 2007; Vaughn and Linan-Thompson 2003).

Just as a runner needs to spend time running to build the stamina needed to compete in a 10-k race, striving readers need to spend significant amounts of time reading if they are to build stamina for connecting to a text for lengthy periods of time.

A helpful tool for building reading stamina and motivation is the VIP strategy on page 101 of this resource.

- Clear goals for building stamina in both reading and writing are essential for striving readers. Just as a runner needs to spend time running to build the stamina needed to compete in a 10-k race, striving readers need to spend significant amounts of time reading if they are to build stamina for connecting to a text for lengthy periods of time. It is significant that the average reading comprehension subtest in state assessments at grade 3 requires sixty to ninety minutes of sustained attention by a reader. For learners who are only used to reading short texts and/or sustaining attention for fifteen minutes of independent reading, the test places an enormous burden on both reading ability and stamina (Boushey and Moser 2006; Calkins, Montgomery, and Santman 1998). As mentors and coaches for striving readers, we need to take this seriously and ensure that striving readers become our partners in setting goals for reading stamina so they can learn to read for extended periods of time. In the Schools that Beat the Odds Studies, the schools that met with the greatest success had all readers, even kindergarteners, reading independently for a minimum of thirty minutes a day—with intermediate grades reading forty-five to sixty minutes a day (Taylor, Pearson, Peterson, and Rodriguez 2003).

- Stamina can be extended with the assistance of individual book boxes or totes in which striving readers have a collection of reading material at their just-right level—right at their fingertips. The benefit is that if a reader tires or finishes a book, it is easy to reach out and grab a new selection. This eliminates avoidance behaviors such as walking to the bookcase to browse for a new title during a time that should be devoted to reading. When developing individual book boxes, it is essential that each personal collection contain an assortment of non-fiction text types (news magazines, leveled selections, or resources on personal topics of interest), as well as fiction selections.

- A postreading partner share can scaffold reading stamina and build intrinsic motivation for attending to text, rather than simply turning pages. A helpful tool for this is the VIP strategy on page 101 of this resource. If you have striving readers mark VIPs as they read independently with the idea that they will be sharing their VIPs with a partner when they finish reading, they are far more likely to attend to the content as they anticipate the partner share.

- In addition to ensuring that striving readers maximize every possible opportunity to read during the school day, options for extending reading outside of the normal school day are well worth considering. There are many programs across the country that link volunteers with readers before and after school as a strategy for adding time with text, or offer after-school enrichment experiences that are loaded with engaging opportunities to read, write, and build valuable background knowledge.

- At-home reading programs, especially where books are provided for learners who may not have access to appropriate reading materials at home are also powerful systems of support for readers who need to spend more time reading. One such program is in Thomasville, North Carolina where readers take home a backpack each night loaded with books at their just-right level and on topics of high interest.

A postreading partner share.

There are many programs across the country that link volunteers with readers before and after school as a strategy for adding time with text or that offer after-school enrichment experiences that are loaded with engaging opportunities to read, write, and build valuable background knowledge.

Access to increased opportunities to read from just-right books is ensured for students in Thomasville, North Carolina. Each night they take home a backpack loaded with books on topics of personal interest.

- Summer reading: Two large-scale studies (Alexander, Entwisle, and Olson 2007; Hayes and Grether 1983) have identified that striving readers may lose three to four months of reading achievement during the summer while other readers typically gain a month of reading growth. This four-month gap is of critical importance as striving readers fall further and further behind each year. Evidence suggests that simply supplying a set of self-selected books to students on the last day of school, signing them up for a home-delivered news magazine each week, or opening the school library one day a week through the summer may be enough to ameliorate this reading loss (McGill-Franzen and Allington 2008; White and Kim 2008). Surprisingly, providing books to read during the summer produced as much reading growth as did sending students to summer school (Allington 2010).

Conferring logs provide a record of observations.

Taking an oral reading record.

Running records scaffold analyses of reading behaviors.

Data-Driven Instruction

- Formative data are the natural by-product of close observation and examination of learning artifacts, and a natural and integral part of every moment of instruction. What is key is that we, as mentors and coaches to striving readers, recognize the importance of what we observe and notice, then take notes, gather work samples, and save evidence that will help us monitor and support the progress of striving readers. Formative data must reside at the heart of instruction for striving readers as it is this evidence of learner progress that informs and shapes expert instruction.

- In schools and classrooms where data drive instruction, you are likely to see teachers collecting informal data within the context of daily instruction, using all available sources of evidence to identify points of progress and areas of need for striving readers. In this kind of learning environment, you might see:

  ✓ A teacher listening in on a partner conversation, then jotting anecdotal notes on a clipboard or in a data notebook.

  ✓ A teacher taking an Oral Reading Record to gather evidence of progress with reading strategies.

  ✓ A teacher taking notes during small-group instruction to record observations of reading strategy use, or a striving reader's attempt to offer critical analysis of a text.

  ✓ Data collection that reflects a broad base of data points ensures that thoughtful consideration is being made for comprehension, word knowledge, fluency, writing, and self-monitoring strategies, all of which are essential to the reading process. As expert instruction must be built on understandings about the full spectrum of reading behaviors that comprise effective, meaning-focused reading, formative assessment must reflect this broad range of behaviors and understandings.

- In schools and classrooms where data drive instruction, progress through reading levels is carefully monitored so every teacher working with a striving reader is continuously aware of which reading levels will best support each reader in instructional settings as well as independent interactions across the curriculum.

- Classroom teachers and specialists share data that they have collected and collaboratively examine both work samples and artifacts of learning to identify points of progress and plan next steps in instruction.

High-Success Reading: Provide Accessible Books and Resources

- Striving readers benefit most from having texts they can read with 99 percent accuracy in their hands for most of the school day. With reading resources in which they experience high levels of success, striving readers have the opportunity to consolidate the skills and strategies they are acquiring, and can focus on comprehending what they have read (Allington 2010; Guthrie and Humenick 2004; Mathes et al. 2005).

- If striving readers are to experience accelerated levels of achievement, they simply must have books at their instructional level, rather than books designed for their grade level. There are far too

When striving readers experience high-success reading all day long, motivation is intrinsic and they develop positive images about themselves as readers.

many classrooms in which striving readers are forced to spend their days listlessly turning the pages of books that are too difficult. Experiences with too-difficult texts reduce reading volume, destroy self-concepts, and limit access to important academic content. Conversely, when striving readers experience high-success reading all day long, motivation is intrinsic and they develop positive images about themselves as readers.

- Kids need books they can read *in every subject area*. This means that schools need to look closely at the books that are available to striving readers in science and social studies—as well as language arts—to ensure that they have the resources they need to create high-success reading across the entire curriculum. This multisourced and multileveled

Kids need books they can read in every subject area. This means that schools need to look closely at the books that are available to striving readers in science and social studies—as well as language arts—to ensure that they have the resources they need to create high-success reading across the entire curriculum.

approach to curriculum results in better content access for striving readers—ensuring that they acquire vital academic content while they continue to grow as readers. When high-success reading permeates every subject area, striving readers will naturally read more and comprehend better as the resources will be comfortable for them to navigate (Allington 2002; Freeman and Freeman 2009; Guthrie and Humenick 2004; Hoyt 2005; Vaughn and Linan-Thompson 2003).

- Classroom libraries are important. High-success reading is facilitated when striving readers have access to books that fascinate and entice. With easy access to books that excite their sense of wonder and lure them into the world of print, striving readers naturally read more. When classroom libraries provide this easy access to interesting books at accessible reading levels, striving readers have the opportunity to make their own choices, explore topics of personal interest, focus on their own questions as readers, and experience self-efficacy. Guthrie and Humenick (2004) conducted a meta-analysis on twenty-two experimental or quasi-experimental studies of classroom reading instruction. They found a huge effect size (ES = 1.64) on reading comprehension achievement for ease of access students had to interesting texts. This is four times as large as the effect size that the National Reading Panel found for systematic phonics instruction on word reading, and roughly ten times the size of the effect size phonics lessons had on reading comprehension.

- During small-group or one to one instruction—when a teacher is close at hand to scaffold and support success in a text that is slightly more difficult than a reader's independent reading level—striving readers can and should be engaged at an instructional reading level. That would be at around 95 percent accuracy—just above the level they can comfortably navigate independently (Pinnell 2006).

High-success reading is facilitated when striving readers have access to books that fascinate and entice.

Emphasize Nonfiction Reading Selections: Slip Fiction to Second Position

- The Common Core State Standards Initiative situates literacy and language development squarely within the content areas. It asserts that it is time to shift from a focus on reading skills and fluency within simple narratives toward reading and writing to gain knowledge and express new understandings with informational texts

(Common Core State Standards 2010; Brozo 2010; Stead and Hoyt 2011). This focus is of vital importance to striving readers as it has been well-proven that reading development is genre specific and that proficiency with fiction texts does not automatically translate to proficiency in the nonfiction texts that comprise the bulk of the reading that learners do throughout schooling and life (Duke and Pearson 2002; Hoyt 2002; Kintsch and Kintsch 2005). It is time to put to rest outdated notions about learning to read before reading to learn. Children can and should be experiencing nonfiction reading opportunities, and lots of them—from the onset of literacy development. It is both natural and effective to learn about the world while you are learning to read—engaging curiosity as well as expanding vocabulary and content knowledge (Brozo and Simpson 2007; Duke and Bennett Armistead 2003).

- Nonfiction, content-based reading can transcend culture and offer concrete support to the development of content knowledge, academic vocabulary, and understandings that will prepare striving readers for the demands of subject area textbooks as well as standardized assessments (Gersten et al. 2008). With nonfiction texts about concrete, real-world subjects such as animals, insects, volcanoes, or weather, striving learners get to read about real things that they may have seen or experienced in some way. They view photographs that offer additional systems of information and language support, and best of all,

With nonfiction texts about concrete, real-world subjects such as animals, insects, volcanoes, or weather, striving learners get to read about real things that they may have seen or experienced in some way.

they get to activate their intrinsic sense of wonder about the world and their own place within it. Evidence suggests that there may be particularly powerful benefits for boys as it has been shown that they prefer informational texts to narrative stories that so often contain culture-specific situations and abstract concepts (Freeman and Freeman 2009; Zambo and Brozo 2009).

- Striving readers experience additional benefits when informational texts are clustered by topic so readers get to experience several books on the same topic. This kind of thematic clustering offers many advantages. In the first book or two on a topic, striving readers establish content-specific vocabulary and develop concepts around a topic. The heavy demands of a new topic are best addressed in books that are at a reader's independent reading level. This ensures that striving readers do not become bogged down by too many challenges at once. As the content and vocabulary of the subject become familiar, the difficulty level of additional books on the same topic can gradually be increased—providing a supported opportunity for a reader to experience increasingly complex texts (Hoyt 2005; Jenkins 2009).

- It is not our intent to suggest that striving readers never experience fiction. Rather, we suggest that it may be time to step back from instructional practices that are based on habit and personal orientation and refocus ourselves on the resources that will best help striving readers experience accelerated development. Fiction was designed to entertain. It was never designed to be a preliminary to informational reading. In adulthood, fiction reading is usually relegated to those slim slivers of time when we can totally relax, slipping away from our busy lives into the amazing world of fiction. We want, and expect, striving readers to learn to love fiction. What we are arguing, however, is the importance of perspective in instruction. Current recommendations from the Common Core State Standards as well as the International Reading Association are that informational texts should comprise the majority of reading done by students in today's classrooms. Fiction reading needs to slip to second position (Common Core State Standards 2010).

- Classroom libraries, bookrooms, and resources purchased for reading instruction should all be closely examined to ensure that the majority of texts offered are informational. It is of additional benefit if the informational topics available in these instructional resources also relate to topics of high interest to striving readers and to the content standards of the grade level.

Nonfiction literacy is of vital importance for striving readers, as it encompasses the majority of reading experiences throughout schooling and in life.

Responsive Instruction: Create Links to What They Know and How They Interact with the World

Responsive instruction is based on the idea that students of diverse cultural and linguistic backgrounds benefit when lessons and instructional supports build on their background knowledge and the strengths they bring from home. The result improves striving students' opportunities for academic success by letting their existing strengths and interests serve as a bridge to the new learning offered by the school. It is essential to note that while cultural differences for immigrant children are clearly evident, they also exist for native English speakers whose home cultures may be different from those of school (Au 2010; Schmidt 2005).

Critical elements of responsive instruction occur when teachers:

1. Set high expectations: Set high goals with your striving readers—expect them to develop the literacies appropriate to their ages and abilities. Model ways to reach goals and continuously monitor progress toward those goals.

2. Activate and value background knowledge. Let striving readers know that you value and appreciate what they already know. Encourage them to make connections. Help them by creating literacy lessons that are culturally relevant so they can connect what may seem like a rigid curriculum to the knowledge and experiences of their lives. When there doesn't seem to be related background knowledge in place, build it with realia and hands-on learning.

3. Float the learning on a sea of talk (Britton 1992). Eliminate hand raising and instead have partners converse about questions you pose so every striving reader has a chance to actively engage, think, and respond to an authentic audience. Seek the healthy hum of engaged conversation! Remember that striving readers of diverse backgrounds may lack the confidence to share an idea spontaneously with the whole class, so distributed discourse, the act of sharing with a partner, may provide an opportunity for striving learners to collect their thoughts and organize the language needed to express their thinking.

Teaching with realia

Have partners converse about questions you pose so every striving reader has a chance to actively engage, think, and respond to an authentic audience.

Active teaching strategies that integrate multimodal responses support culturally responsive instruction.

Involve striving readers in a variety of reading, writing, listening, speaking, and viewing experiences throughout each lesson.

It is often a good sign when a visitor finds it difficult to spot the teacher, as it means the teacher is not at the front of the room, but rather deeply engrossed interacting with individuals and small groups.

4. Use active teaching strategies. Involve striving readers in a variety of reading, writing, listening, speaking, and viewing experiences throughout each lesson. Invite striving readers to sketch as a way of representing what they have learned and understand. Provide manipulatives so they can physically manipulate elements related to the target learning. Have them dramatize the way that magma flows through a volcanic chamber or the attitude a character is displaying during a critical scene in a book.

5. Redefine your role in the lesson. Become a facilitator—present information; briefly give directions; summarize, and get kids talking! Then, spend your time working with small groups, pairs, and individuals. It is often a good sign when a visitor finds it difficult to spot the teacher, as it means the teacher is not at the front of the room, but rather deeply engrossed interacting with individuals and small groups.

6. Focus on learner engagement. Build instructional time around groups and pairs. This is a low-anxiety situation for striving readers that helps them increase engagement, language use, and academic achievement.

7. Involve families of striving readers as partners in the learning of their children. Families from diverse ethnic and cultural backgrounds or lower socioeconomic situations often feel a separation between home and school. Reach out to them—make connections; this will narrow the gap and increase positive attitudes toward school.

Build instructional time around groups and pairs.

Involve families of striving readers as partners in the learning of their children.

Tables and desks are organized in clusters to support conversation with partners and teams.

The learning environment should be inviting.

Walls are not merely decorated, but filled with tools that support striving readers.

A Responsive Lesson

In a lesson about the physics of sound, a teacher began by bringing in a variety of musical instruments. She demonstrated their use and discussed the vibrations of the strings on a guitar, the vibration of the skin on a drum, and the vibration that occurs when the plates of a tambourine clang together. Students talked with partners and then drew diagrams to illustrate their observations of the sounds produced by each instrument. Vocabulary was then introduced with words such as sound waves, vibration, and frequency—each being defined using the musical instruments. The homework assignment was to bring in musical instruments, recorded music, or other items that created sound, such as a bell, as a means for applying the new vocabulary and concepts.

This example lesson was culturally responsive as it provided striving readers with active involvement and immediate channels through which to connect their prior knowledge, their observations, and their home experiences. It also provided multiple systems of communication (viewing, listening, talking, writing, and personal exploration) to ensure that every learner could find a pathway to understanding.

Learner-Focused Environments: Set the Stage for Engagement, Interaction, and Independence

Environments, both in the regular classroom and in intervention settings, set the stage for accelerated learning. When entering an environment that is designed to support striving readers, it is helpful to consider the following features:

- Are there tables or desks organized in clusters to support conversation with partners and teams?

- Is the learning environment highly organized with a place for everything? This is highly important for striving readers as many are greatly affected by disorganization and clutter. The room should be inviting—a model of organization and beauty. This may mean that teachers need to rethink storage of their supplies to ensure that supplies and "to do" piles are out of sight.

- Look closely at the walls. They should not be "decorated" but rather filled with tools that support striving readers as readers, writers, and thinkers. Learning targets such as strategies should be clearly posted

There should be areas for gathering the entire class up close to view an enlarged text or an interactive whiteboard.

so that current curricular emphases are visible to students, colleagues, and community members.

- There should be areas for gathering the entire class up close to view an enlarged text or an interactive whiteboard, or have a community meeting.

- There should be areas for meeting with small groups and individuals.

- Movement around the room should be comfortable.

- The teacher desk should be either at the back of the room or nonexistent.

- Space should be allocated for learning, rather than teacher storage.

 # Instructional Alignment: Classroom Teachers and Interventionists Operate as a Team

- Classroom teachers and interventionists must begin to see themselves as a well-coordinated team focused on shared goals. Like the pit crew at the Indianapolis 500, this team should operate at maximum efficiency to ensure that the "race car" gets back on the track as quickly as possible. This means that they need to talk about standards, about reading levels, about content goals, and reading strategies. They need to share the formative data that they each collect and have discussions reflecting on the response of each striving reader to the scaffolds and supports they are providing. Research indicates a substantial benefit

The learning environment is highly organized, with a place for everything.

when lessons provided by interventionists are well coordinated with classroom reading instruction (Borman, Wong, Hedges, and D'Agostino 2003) and united by content-specific units of study.

- It is also essential to understand that there is no theory or evidence that striving readers need to be taught a different reading curriculum. There is evidence, however, that when striving readers are offered a different curriculum—uncoordinated or detached from the focus points of the regular classroom—reading development slows (Allington 2010).

- Evidence suggests that relatively few students continue to struggle when careful instructional alignment includes expert classroom instruction and reading resources that offer high-success reading experiences all day long; the volume of reading is increased; and additional small-group instruction, tightly coordinated with the thematic content of the classroom, is available (Mathes et al. 2005; Vellutino et al. 1996).

Space should be allocated for learning, rather than teacher storage.

PART ONE

Solutions for Navigating Nonfiction

PART

1

Solutions for Navigating Nonfiction

Scaffolds for Understanding Nonfiction

Nonfiction print fills our lives. Everywhere we look there are newspapers, magazines, directions, street signs, recipes, letters, Internet sites, and educational resources brimming with inviting content about the real world. Yet, research suggests that even though informational texts comprise the majority of texts read by literate adults, far too few children are taught explicit strategies for reading nonfiction (Jeong, Gaffney, and Choi 2010; Duke 2000; Freeman and Freeman 2009). Although nonfiction reading is important for all students, it has special significance for striving readers. To be successful in school and in the workplace, striving readers must learn to navigate nonfiction sources with confidence and purpose—to gain control over the content, structures, language forms, and visual features that comprise the heart of informational texts. In addition, our new Common Core Standards (2010) place a major emphasis on increasing the quantity and complexity of the nonfiction texts students at all grade levels will be required to read and comprehend, making it more important than ever that striving readers are empowered with a broad base of nonfiction strategies (Schwartz 2006; Common Core State Standards 2010; Hoyt 2009b; Vaughn and Linan-Thompson 2004).

It is also significant to note that we, as coaches and mentors for striving readers, must ensure that they learn strategically—spontaneously attending to content-based vocabulary and applying meaning-seeking strategies so they can monitor and extend their own comprehension. We must also ensure that readers who need additional scaffolds for learning receive explicit instruction in strategies for retaining content, determining importance, and using writing as a tool for processing and communicating information (Short and Fitzsimmons 2007; Pearson 2008; Roller 1996).

It is helpful to remember that in childhood, understanding builds from concrete experience. Concepts, understanding, and language are best acquired through real experiences with real things. When striving readers get to touch, think, talk, and wonder, they feel a stronger connection to their learning and surge forward with a powerful intrinsic motivation. For these reasons, nonfiction is a perfect support system for special education learners, students learning English as an additional language, children of poverty, and those with limited academic language and experience (Stead and Hoyt 2011a; Vaughn, Gersten, and Chard 2000; Au 2010). Nonfiction experiences invite language use while helping striving readers to access important content in science, social studies, health, and so on.

As mentors and coaches for vulnerable learners, we believe the following points are essential to success for striving readers of nonfiction.

1. Select the best nonfiction resources for striving readers. When nonfiction selections are used for the purpose of gathering facts for writing, then photographs, diagrams, and other supportive visuals are important information sources—no matter what the material's reading level. In this case, giving striving readers access to a wide range of text difficulty levels may be appropriate. It is amazing how much information they can glean from well-crafted visuals in books and magazines.

   If the purpose, however, is reading instruction, the reading level must be accessible and comfortable for the reader. It has been well proven that immersing striving readers in books that are too difficult can actually cause a regression in their development (Allington 2006). For reading instruction with nonfiction selections, we highly recommend selecting books at a level your striving readers can read with fluency and confidence. When the reading level is comfortable, striving readers can focus on navigating the content and applying meaning-seeking strategies. The resources that may best support your striving readers are likely to be those designed for guided reading and are organized around alphabetic or Reading Recovery leveling systems. Basal anthologies, unfortunately, have fewer high-quality visuals, fewer text features, and a more limited range of text types than individual books that are designed for guided reading instruction (Moss 2003; Baker, Dreher, and Guthrie 2000; Cooper, Chard, and Kieger 2006).

2. Create companion collections by gathering books on the same topic representing a range of reading levels. Research suggests that striving readers benefit from multiple text experiences related to the same topic because the core academic vocabulary they build enables them to read increasingly more difficult texts related to the topic. With concepts and key vocabulary in hand, striving readers who might normally read at a given level can move into more complex reading selections on the same topic (Hoyt 2005; Kendall and Khoun 2005; Taberski 2011; Freeman and Freeman 2009; Klingner, Vaughn, and Boardman 2007).

Companion collections build interest and deeper concept development.

When creating companion collections, it might be helpful to ask yourself the following questions:

- Are there multiple copies of books that can be included and used during small-group strategy instruction?

- Have I included some single copies of books that can be used for individual reading, research, or read-alouds?

- Could I include any articles from newsmagazines?

- Have I included books on tape so that all students can access information in which they are interested?

- Have I collected books with a wide range of readability so that all students can find access to the topic and still read books at their just-right level?

- Can I organize this set so that another teacher could use it, too?

- Are there books in our school book room that could be temporarily added to the set and then returned when the unit of study is complete?

- Do I have access to any textbooks that could be used for this set?

3. Think aloud as you read from nonfiction selections, letting striving readers observe closely as you crack open your thinking and invite them to listen in (Harvey and Goudvis 2007; Keene and Zimmerman 2007; Hoyt 2007). A think-aloud with nonfiction (see also the Thinking Aloud solution to Question #1) might sound something like: *In this Seymour Simon book about tornadoes, the funnel looks like a huge elephant trunk hanging from a cloud. Picture it! Elephant trunks don't hang straight down, they move around, weaving as the elephant walks or reaches out for things the elephant wants. Based on what it says in the book, I can picture the funnel of the tornado moving and shifting, bending and twisting as it sways between the cloud and the ground. It is full of motion! I didn't understand that before. Read the next paragraph with a partner and think together. Tell each other about your thinking as you read.*

Explicit modeling and thinking aloud show striving readers how to navigate nonfiction texts.

- Demonstrate how to read a small amount of text, then pause to reflect out loud, identifying facts that are important as compared to those that are details. Next, show your striving readers how to jot a key word or phrase on an individual sticky note to remind yourself of an important fact. As information is gathered, model how to arrange sticky notes in a logical order and tell a thinking partner why you chose them.

- Model how to sketch as you collect information, infusing details into a drawing and adding labels to help yourself remember descriptive vocabulary. Then, provide opportunities for striving readers to try the strategies themselves with the goal of sharing their informational sketches and labels with learning partners.

- Show striving readers how you self-monitor understanding. They need to see how you slow down to reread a confusing passage, pause to look more closely at a visual, look at the glossary to clarify the meaning of a key word.

- Bring readers in close and show them a variety of ways to work with a challenging word. Let them listen in as you think aloud about reading on to gain meaning from the passage or try to insert a synonym that makes sense. Cue them to "listen closely" as you chunk a word into meaningful units to see if that helps you make sense of the passage.

4. Model strategies for navigating nonfiction selections. Show striving readers *how* to move through a nonfiction text as you demonstrate how to investigate a table of contents, review the index, skim the headings, and so on. Tell readers that reading nonfiction is a bit like

navigating a car. Drivers usually know their destination, which street they will start on, and where they are going to turn. These navigational strategies make it easier to get to where they are going. To read fiction, you simply start on page 1. Navigation isn't difficult.

In nonfiction, however, you need to navigate! First, you identify your destination—your purpose for reading. Then, identify which portions of the book are most likely to provide information that you need. For example: *Watch as I begin to navigate this book, I know that I am searching for information on ____. So, I will first look in the index to see if ____ is listed. If it is, I can go directly to the page that will assist me. If the index doesn't help, my plan is to look at the table of contents. If that still doesn't help me find the pages I need, I will skim the headings to find one that is likely to be about ____. Readers of informational texts need to have a reading plan so they can navigate effectively as they read. Remember, in nonfiction, you don't always start on page 1* (Hoyt 2002).

5. Link strategies used in fiction with strategies used in nonfiction. Striving readers often feel overwhelmed so it can be very reassuring to see that many of the strategies they use in fiction selections also work well in informational passages. Clue them into a wonderful secret: Rules about phonics, chunking words, and grammar all apply in nonfiction, too! Metacognitive strategies such as inferring, questioning, summarizing, determining importance, using sensory images, self-monitoring, and synthesizing also work in nonfiction selections. As coaches, we just need to make it explicitly clear to striving students when and how to activate these strategies with informational texts. As noted by Vaughn, Gersten, and Chard (2000), there is significant evidence suggesting that many children with learning disabilities experience poor comprehension because they are failing to read strategically and to spontaneously monitor their understanding of what is being read.

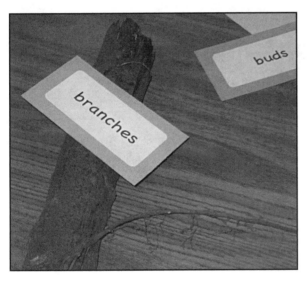

Real things, when combined with visual supports, aid in concept development and expansion of academic vocabulary.

6. Plan before-reading experiences as interactions with real things, with richly detailed photographs, or with carefully scaffolded concept and vocabulary-building experiences. Prereading supports are critical in helping striving readers build content-specific concepts and language. With enticing photographs and real objects, language flows naturally as learners share their observations, their questions, and their prior knowledge. It is significant to note that evidence suggests that interactive dialogue and student-generated questions have a highly positive impact on learning for striving readers (Freeman and Freeman 2009; Allington 2009; Keene 2007; Kendall and Khoun 2005).

7. Have striving readers draw and write about nonfiction understandings. We know that reading and writing are reciprocal processes and that when readers write and sketch, they reconsider and reflect upon information they have learned as they re-present the content through drawings and in their own words. When striving readers have opportunities to write about what they have learned in their reading, academic vocabulary is immediately used and content retention is supported (Pearson 2008; Marzano 2004; Allington 2006).

8. Teach striving readers the features of nonfiction texts so they understand how to engage with the features and use them as supports to understanding. Informational texts have many unique features that are designed to support readers in navigating through resources and provide reader-friendly access to content (Rea and Mercuri 2006; Vacca and Vacca 2008). When readers see explicit demonstrations of how to use nonfiction features, they realize that taking time to examine a labeled diagram before reading a text can make comprehension easier. They learn that boldfaced text is designed to signal a reader and draw attention to important words and ideas. And they learn that photographs can be rich sources of detail and factual information. Fostering the use of text features enhances a reader's ability to comprehend throughout his life.

Nonfiction Text Features also appears on the CD.

Nonfiction Text Features

Communicate Information Visually	Draw Attention to Important Ideas and Concepts
Photograph	Title/headline
Illustration	Heading
Diagram	Subheading
Chart	Arrow
Graph	Boldface
Table	Caption
Flowchart	Table of contents
Storyboard	Glossary
Map	Index
Legend/key	Text box
Cross section	Bullet
Cutaway	Callout
Timeline	

PROMPTS to Support Striving Learners

Nonfiction Text

Prompts to Support Learning
Nonfiction Text also appears on the CD.

If You Notice This:	*You Might Prompt This:*
➪ **The reader opens a nonfiction book and immediately begins to focus on the words.**	• With nonfiction resources, it is important to preview the pictures, check for labeled diagrams, and think about what you know about the topic. Let's begin with a close look at the pictures. • In nonfiction, we don't always start on page 1. We can think of a question we have about the topic, then check the index and table of contents to see what part of the book is likely to answer the question. In nonfiction, sometimes you start in the middle of the book.
➪ **The reader focuses on decoding rather than thinking about the topic.**	• [Cover the text with a piece of paper.] Let's look closely at this picture. Look for details and describe what you see. What words would tell about this picture? What words will you expect to see when you start reading? As you list the words you expect to see, I will jot them down for you. • The topic is _____. What do you know about this topic? Think of a question you hope will be answered as you read today, then read to see if your answer is in the book.
➪ **The reader does not take time to consciously activate prior knowledge before reading.**	• [Before reading] Look at the cover of this book and think: What do you already know about this topic? If you were to draw a picture about this topic, what details would you include? What labels would you add to your illustration? • [Guide the reader in previewing photographs and visuals.] Think about connections you might make to this topic: Have you seen other books about this topic? Have you had a personal experience with this topic? Perhaps you have seen something on television about this?
➪ **The reader has limited prior knowledge on the topic.**	• [Provide realia, video clips, and photographs. If those are not available, do a sketch of your own, explaining about the subject as you sketch.] Thinking partners, put your heads together. What are you noticing? What do you see? Tell each other what you are learning. • Do a sketch of your own. Be sure to add lots of labels. Sketches are a great way to hold onto information so you can remember what you are learning.

L. Hoyt, K. Davis, J. Olson, and K. Boswell, Solutions for Reading Comprehension, © 2011. Portsmouth, NH: Heinemann.
May be photocopied for classroom use only.

continues

Nonfiction Text (cont.)

Prompts to Support Learning
Nonfiction Text also appears on the CD.

If You Notice This:	You Might Prompt This:
⇨ **The reader is challenged by the content-specific vocabulary in the passage.**	• One of the things readers do to help themselves understand nonfiction is spend time thinking about vocabulary before they begin reading. Let's preview the pictures and use these sticky notes to jot down words that will be important to remember as we read about _____. [Use one word per sticky note.] Another trick is to add a little sketch next to the word to remind yourself what it means. I will identify some words that I think will really be important, but I am counting on you to identify important words as well. • Are there clues in the sentence or illustration that might help you? • Have you checked the glossary?
⇨ **The reader reads too much text without pausing to reflect.**	• Notice that I have placed sticky notes at various places in this book. These are like stop signs. Every time you come to a sticky note, it is your job to stop reading and think about what you just read. With nonfiction, we need pauses to decide what is important and decide if we understand or if we need to read the section again.
⇨ **The reader does not attend to nonfiction text features such as headings, boldfaced words, captions, and so on.**	• Before you begin reading, I am going to ask you to do a scavenger hunt and search through the pages for boldfaced words. Each time you find one, think hard. Why is that word bold? What makes that particular word important to this topic? [Repeat for headings, captions, and so on.] • Do you agree with the choice of bold words the author made on this page? If you were the author, would you have selected any other words to show as boldfaced type?

Prompts to Support Learning
Nonfiction Text also appears on the CD.

If You Notice This:	*You Might Prompt This:*
⇨ **The reader does not determine importance while reading.**	• What is the most important idea or event? • Which of these ideas (pointing to several) are the most important? Let's sort them by importance. • Here are some strips of sticky note material. There aren't a lot of strips, just a few. When you come to a fact or idea that you think is very important, mark it with a strip. When you finish reading, be ready to tell why you selected that fact as being a very important point.
⇨ **The reader sounds out every word.**	• It is important to be sure that reading sounds like talking. The words should flow together so that they sound smooth and expressive. Listen as I read these sentences. Now, it is your turn. Read the same sentences I just read. • There are lots of ways to work with words that are tricky: You can take time to think about the topic. You can look at the beginning sound and think about what would make sense in this sentence. You can find a little word in the big word or break it into chunks. Once you think you know the word, then go back to the beginning of the sentence and read it again with fluency. Reading should sound smooth—just like people talking.
⇨ **The reader focuses on details rather than main ideas.**	• Nonfiction is filled with facts, so readers need to think about how the facts connect and focus on main ideas. We have written some details on sticky notes. Let's group them together and see if we can identify some main ideas. When we identify the main idea, we can write it at the top of the page and put the sticky notes that go with it underneath. Keep in mind, there may be several main ideas.

L. Hoyt, K. Davis, J. Olson, and K. Boswell, Solutions for Reading Comprehension, © 2011. Portsmouth, NH: Heinemann. May be photocopied for classroom use only.

How Do I Scaffold Prior Knowledge and Vocabulary with Nonfiction?

Side-by-Side Observation: Emilio

Emilio is a third grader recently released from direct English language services. We meet with him frequently to ensure that supports are in place as he makes this transition. While reading informational texts, Emilio asks many questions and his facial expression indicates confusion. His visible confusion suggests that he expects the text to make sense—a good sign! Emilio's running questions indicate that he is trying to self-monitor his comprehension by questioning the text continuously. Deeper probing with a Nonfiction Retell Checklist and an Informational Text Strategy Observation indicates that Emilio would benefit from an emphasis on activating prior knowledge and utilizing content-specific vocabulary.

Formative Assessment Tools

⇨ Running record

⇨ Nonfiction Retell Checklist, page 183

⇨ Informational Text Strategy Observation, page 166

Careful coaching with nonfiction selections sets the stage for success across the curriculum.

We Notice . . . In reflecting on formative assessments, observations, and an interview with Emilio, we notice:

- Emilio has strong accuracy and reads with expression in fiction selections.

- He asks questions about content vocabulary and concepts, suggesting that he is attempting to self-monitor his own comprehension.

- On many topics, Emilio lacks prior knowledge and the vocabulary needed to comprehend informational passages. He would benefit from experiences that show him how to activate prior knowledge and focus on content-specific vocabulary.

- There is marked improvement in his comprehension when he gets to read several books on the same topic.

We Will Try . . . To help Emilio and students like him think about what he already knows and more effectively engage with prior knowledge and vocabulary, we will support him with the following:

Word Prediction page 34	Thinking Aloud page 36	Word Sort page 39	Guided Preview page 42

 Small Group · Partners · One-to-One	Whole Class · Small Group · Partners	Whole Class · Small Group · Partners	Whole Class · Small Group · Partners · Independent

Additional Solutions to Consider

Realia page 38	Interactive Sentences page 41

Whole Class · Small Group · Partners	Small Group · Partners · Independent

Small Group

Partners

One-to-One

Word Prediction

Word prediction is a highly supportive strategy that engages striving readers in actively accessing prior knowledge. In this *solution*, the teacher guides an individual or a small group in previewing a text—examining the title, cover, photographs, headings, and so on. (It is helpful to have striving readers cover running text with their hands or a sheet of paper.) As readers examine the resource, invite them to predict words they expect to see when they begin to read. With each word they predict, it is important that learners tell *why* they expect their word to appear.

An example for a book on sharks: *I predict that the word fin will be in this book because I know that sharks have a large fin on their back that can show above the water. I predict that the word teeth will be in this book because I know that sharks have teeth so they can eat their prey.*

The list of words provided by the students is a perfect opportunity for assessment as a quick scan of the vocabulary generated by the students shows what they already know. Then, the teacher can suggest additional words for the chart to round out the academic vocabulary most needed to comprehend the content.

As you record the predicted words, be sure to ask students why they think they will find that word in the text.

Steps for *Word Prediction*

1. In a small group setting, demonstrate how you look at the pictures, diagrams, and headings of a text, then begin predicting words you expect to see when you read. Scaffold your striving readers by using a language stem such as: *I predict that the word _____ will be in the book because _____.*

2. Distribute copies of the book to partner pairs and have them begin predicting words, making sure that they also tell why they think each word is important to the topic.

3. Record predicted words on a chart.

4. Analyze the words students have provided and select a few additional words that you believe are essential to support the content. As you add words to the chart, use the language stem and tell why the word is important. Then, have your striving readers find a page in the book where they think your word would fit. For a book such as *Spiders* by Gail Gibbons, the students are not likely to predict words such as *spinnerets*, *arachnid*, *egg sac*, and so on, so these would be helpful additions for step 4.

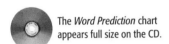

Word Prediction

Reader_____ Book/Article_____ Date_____

Before Reading

Words I predict will be in this book	I think this word is important because	(✓) Check if you find the word in the book. You might also want to record the page number.

After Reading: The words listed below are additional words I found while reading that I believe are important to this topic.

Other important words	I think this word is important because

The *Word Prediction* chart appears full size on the CD.

5. As students read the selection, challenge them to try to find the words on the Word Prediction chart and mark them with a strip of sticky note material on the pages of their book or magazine.

6. Provide time for partners to reflect on their word predictions and share where they found words in the book.

7. As striving learners gain confidence, have them make word predictions independently.

As partners discuss their word predictions, vocabulary is strengthened and prior knowledge is activated.

Thinking Aloud: Activate Prior Knowledge and Connections

Whole Class OR **Small Group**

Partners

Think-alouds provide opportunities to model and invite striving readers to peek into the thinking of a proficient reader. Although think-alouds could focus on any dimension of thoughtful, reflective literacy, in this *solution* the focus is on tapping prior knowledge and making connections. The goal of the think-aloud is to demonstrate conscious activation of prior knowledge and to make connections that directly relate to the text. An important by-product of conscious reflection and thinking aloud is that metacognitive awareness is heightened and students become more aware of what they do and do not know. An example (using *Born to Be a Butterfly* by Karen Wallace, a Dorling Kindersley Reader):

Anchor charts when combined with explicit think-alouds provide multifaceted layers of support for striving readers.

As I read, listen to how I use prior knowledge and make connections to understand. I will think out loud so you know what is going on inside of my head as I use my prior knowledge. The first pages say that the butterfly has red stripes. As I think about butterflies I have seen, I don't think I have ever seen one that is red. I have seen yellow stripes, but not red. It says the butterfly flits from flower to flower. Using my prior knowledge again, I can really picture this! I remember seeing butterflies land on flowers. They were so light, the stem of the flower didn't even bend. My prior knowledge really helps. Next, the book says the butterfly is looking for a leaf to lay her egg. I don't have any prior knowledge about butterfly eggs. I have never seen one. I am going to read this part very carefully to see what I can learn about the eggs. Then I will have new information to add to my prior knowledge about butterflies. It's your turn. Read the next section with your partner and then think aloud for each other. Share any prior knowledge that helps you understand. Also, tell each other when you do not have prior knowledge, so you need to read with extra care.

Steps for *Thinking Aloud: Activate Prior Knowledge and Connections*

1. Using a nonfiction text for which you have prior knowledge and are able to make connections, think aloud as you actively link prior knowledge to the content you are reading. Read small sections of text, then

pause to think aloud about the prior knowledge—if any—that will help you. Tell your students when you come to a passage for which you have no prior knowledge and must read with extra care to understand.

2. Make sure that striving readers realize that this is not a time to tell a story about a memory. The goal is to tap into experiences and connections that assist in building better comprehension.

3. Read another passage and have partners think about their own prior knowledge. Have they had an experience or done some reading that will help them understand the passage?

4. As your striving readers demonstrate understanding of the process, have partner pairs work together to read short amounts of text, then share available prior knowledge and connections with each other.

Additional statements to fuel awareness of prior knowledge:

Statements That Activate Prior Knowledge and Connections
Once I saw . . .
When I was_____, I noticed . . .
This reminds me of . . .
I never heard of this before . . .
Once I read that . . .
I wonder if this is like . . .
On television I saw . . .
I saw a photograph that . . .
This is new to me. Do you have prior knowledge about this?
This reminds me of a book that I read.

 OR

Whole Class   **Small Group**

Partners

Make It Concrete with Realia

When striving readers lack prior knowledge on a topic, it is essential that we find ways to provide it using real experiences and realia. Learning becomes more relevant and meaningful when richly detailed photographs and experiences with real things are used to power up schema and conceptual understanding. In this *solution*, realia, concrete objects, and experiences support vocabulary development and knowledge that is essential for comprehending nonfiction (Short and Fitzsimmons 2007; Kluth 2007; Vacca and Vacca 2008; McGregor 2007).

Realia in the form of real objects, high-quality visuals, and video clips broaden understanding and support striving readers as they interact with nonfiction selections.

Steps for *Make It Concrete with Realia*

1. Introduce a topic using video clips, photographs, and real objects. For example, when introducing the topic of trees, you might provide real bark, leaves, pine needles, and pine cones for students to see, touch, and smell. Explaining and orally labeling each object as you present it helps students make the connection between the object and the word.

2. When using actual objects, provide an opportunity for students to touch them, examine them with magnifying glasses, and talk with partners about their observations.

3. Use prepared vocabulary cards that label the pictures and realia.

4. Encourage students to create labeled diagrams and sketches to help them remember details and vocabulary. We suggest using a Learning Log, which consists of blank or lined paper folded in half and stapled into a book. Students can collect information on a topic in the Learning Log and refer back to it as the study of the topic continues.

5. Give partners an opportunity to share their observations, identify important vocabulary, or share their sketches and labeled diagrams.

Word Sort and Wonder

Word sorts and student-generated questions are powerful partners for front-loading vocabulary and motivating striving readers. We recommend this combination when content is challenging and students need a sturdy foundation for new vocabulary and concepts. To prepare this *solution*, select nine to twelve words and phrases related to the target content and place each within a rectangle. (*Tip*: Insert the words into a table within your word processor then enlarge the font and print enough for your students.) Then have partners cluster words that they can connect in a meaningful way. In a passage about frogs, *jump* and *powerful legs* can be matched and a statement generated such as *Frogs use their powerful legs to jump*. It is important to model how to sort the words and then make statements that highlight the reason these words are a good match (Hoyt 2002).

| jump | powerful legs |

Next, students generate questions with I Wonder statements (Hoyt 2003) focused on their word pairings. An example: *I wonder how it is that frogs can jump so far?* This sets a purpose for reading, sparks curiosity, and engages striving readers in energetic discussions related to the content.

Steps for *Word Sort and Wonder*

1. Preparation: Preview the text, selecting nine to twelve words and phrases that are key to comprehension. Type and print out words and phrases for each pair of students.

Word sorts help striving readers see links between concepts and ideas.

Note: The number of words will vary depending on topic, level of text difficulty, and student instructional level. Students should be familiar with at least half of the words, and visuals may be added to the cards to add additional scaffolding.

2. In a whole-class or small-group setting, model how to select two rectangles and generate a statement that shows how they can be meaningfully linked. You may want to place rectangles on a chart and then draw a circle around the pairings. Be sure to model the use of vocabulary that you think will be particularly challenging to your students as this will provide a context and scaffold meaning.

3. Have students work in partnerships to sort the words and phrases into pairs and practice generating linking statements.

4. Invite partners to review their sorted words and generate I Wonder questions.

Sample Word Sort for Plant Parts			
trunk	food travels	stores food	leaves
bark	underground	food enters	roots
protects trunk	sun	water	air

Adapted from Linda Hoyt, Revisit, Reflect, Retell, *Updated Edition, © 2009. Portsmouth, NH: Heinemann.*

Content words and phrases are typed, cut apart, and given to each pair of students.

Small Group

Partners

Independent

Interactive Sentences

Striving readers often have trouble remembering the new learning in informational texts because they haven't taken adequate time to interact with the content and vocabulary before reading. In Interactive Sentences, individual students are presented with one sentence or fact from a reading selection. Each student reads the sentence to a partner and listens as the partner paraphrases. That student, in turn, listens to his partner's sentence and paraphrases what *he* hears. Then students move around the room at the teacher's command, form new partners, and share their sentences once more. As students circulate to hear and paraphrase a variety of sentences, they gain a greater understanding of the content and are ready to read the selection with their prior knowledge activated. This *solution* is highly engaging as students get to stand up, move around, and use lots of language as they paraphrase (Kletzien 2009). The result is that striving readers enter a new reading selection powered up with familiar vocabulary and sentences. As they begin to read, you can hear them saying: "There it is. That is my sentence," or "There's Alina's sentence!"

Steps for *Interactive Sentences*

1. In advance of the session, extract sentences from a book that will be read by the group. If you have five students in the group, extract five different sentences, one for each learner. For example, if the group will be reading a book about frogs, you might extract these sentences from the text: *1. A frog's skin is pink and wet. 2. Big eyes help the frogs find food. 3. Frogs have a long, sticky tongue. 4. In winter, frogs look for a warm, safe place to hibernate. 5. Frog eggs stick together in a big blob of slimy jelly called frog spawn.*

2. Gather a small group of learners. Present each student with one of the sentences.

3. Invite partners to meet and share their sentences with each other. After Partner A reads her sentence, Partner B paraphrases and restates the sentence.

Interactive Sentences help striving readers become familiar with concepts and vocabulary before they enter a text. The result—confidence and high-quality comprehension.

4. Next, Partner B reads his sentence and Partner A paraphrases.

5. Then, individuals move on to interact with a new partner and a new sentence.

6. Once all students have interacted, invite individuals to draw and/or write to summarize what they can remember from the various sentences.

7. Finally, present the small group with the original passage from which all sentences have been extracted. Allow students to read the text and discuss their thinking with a partner.

Guided Preview

Striving readers have been shown to gravitate directly to the running text in nonfiction, when they really should always begin with photographs, visuals, headings, and so on (Klingner, Vaughn, and Boardman 2007; Pearson 1999; Rea and Mercuri 2006). A Guided Preview helps students understand the power of slowing down and approaching informational texts thoughtfully—directing their attention to the visuals and text features before they begin to read. The idea of a Guided Preview is to model how to approach a text, showing striving readers that sometimes you start at the beginning and other times you start at the index—the end—to quickly search for an answer to a question. In this *solution*, helping striving readers understand that you navigate informational texts differently from fiction is an essential goal in coaching and mentoring them toward higher levels of achievement with nonfiction.

In a Guided Preview, striving readers learn to take time with visuals, activate prior knowledge, and examine text features.

Guided Preview also appears on the CD.

Steps for *Guided Preview*

1. Using a text that is highly visible for your students, begin a think-aloud focused on *how* to preview a nonfiction text. Some key ideas to demonstrate might include:

   - Scan pictures.

   - Read headings.

   - Ask questions and wondering.

   - Read the table of contents and pick a section that sounds interesting.

   - Identify a question then check the index. Dip into the text to answer a question, then ask another one and repeat the process.

   - Be sure that striving readers are noticing that you aren't starting on page 1 and reading every page in order—yet.

   As your readers demonstrate understanding of the preview process, provide them with copies of the Guided Preview and have them preview a book with a partner.

2. Gather readers back together to talk about what they learned while previewing.

Name of Reader_____ Text_____ Date_____

Before Reading

Skim (look quickly through the book) and think . . .

What kind of reading is this? What is the topic? _____

What challenges should I be prepared for? _____

What supports are here? Is there a table of contents, boldfaced words, heading, photographs? _____

_____

Prior knowledge that I bring to this reading selection includes _____

_____

Based on my preview of this book, my questions are:

_____

_____

_____

As I previewed the photographs, diagrams, and other visuals, I noticed that _____

_____

_____

Words that I predict are likely to appear in this reading selection include _____

_____

I am most excited to read and learn more about: _____

_____

_____

_____

How Can I Help Striving Learners Remember the Big Ideas?

Side-by-Side Observation: Peter

While listening to Peter read a nonfiction selection, we observe that he is not attending to text features such as bold print, photographs, and illustrations. When we ask him about what he has read, his retell includes minimal details and does not include much of the valuable information found in the visuals, captions, and headings. To make sure that this wasn't a single episode caused by a mismatch between Peter and the text, we confer with Peter several times while using an Informational Text Strategy Observation (see page 166) to gather additional formative data. As suspected, ongoing data confirm that Peter would benefit from additional support in strategies for engaging with nonfiction text in a way that helps him attend to and retain pertinent information.

Formative Assessment Tools

⇨ Nonfiction Retell Checklist, page 183

⇨ Informational Text Strategy Observation, page 166

⇨ Individual Conference Notes, page 151

Close observation provides important information about the ways in which striving readers interact with nonfiction.

We Notice . . . In reflecting on our formative assessments and individual conferences with Peter, we notice:

- He tends to ignore text features.

- He has limited recall of information from nonfiction texts.

We Will Try . . . To help students like Peter reach for deeper understanding and content retention, we will try the following:

Sketch, Label, Share page 46	Questioning page 48	Jot It Down page 50	Bookmarks page 55

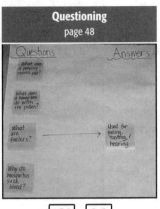

Small Group · Partners · Independent · Small Group · Partners · Small Group · Partners · Whole Class · Small Group · Independent

Additional Solutions to Consider

Text Structure page 52	Frame page 57	Text Features page 60

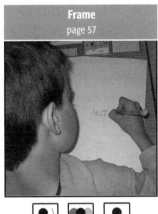

Whole Class · Small Group · Partners · Whole Class · Small Group · Independent · Whole Class · Small Group · Partners

Small Group

Partners

Independent

Sketch, Label, Share

In Sketch, Label, Share, striving readers pause during their reading to create quick sketches and accompanying labels (using key words or phrases). These visual representations support content retention, boost comprehension, and strengthen writing skills (Keene and Zimmerman 2007). In addition, the explicit nature of this *solution* scaffolds those students who are acquiring English, are experiencing language deficits, or would benefit from additional visual supports. Although there are many variations to this strategy (Siegel 1985; Hoyt 2009b; Willis 2007; Marzano 2004), all are firmly grounded in the research that suggests that students remember more when they have taken the time to process new information and visually represent their thinking.

Visual representations support content retention and scaffold language use.

As with all supportive instruction, teacher modeling is key. While reading a nonfiction book during a read-aloud or shared reading experience, pause frequently to think out loud about the information you have just learned. Then, make a quick sketch on chart paper showing the new learning. Use stick figures, arrows, and labels to represent your thinking.

When reading biographies, historical recounts, or a description of a life cycle, you might draw arrows between sketches and have the sketches flow horizontally. On the other hand, if you are reading a text that explores cycles such as the water cycle or a life cycle of a plant or animal, you might show students how you create your sketches in such a way that they form a circle connected by arrows.

TIP

Work in one color so that you make clear that a *sketch* is different from an *illustration*.

Steps for *Sketch, Label, Share*

1. Working with a small group of striving readers, present partner pairs with copies of a nonfiction text that is at an independent reading level. Prepare the text with preplaced, blank sticky notes as stop points.

2. Model how to read up to a sticky note, then stop and create a quick sketch to capture the content, including labels with key words or phrases. Refer to the sketch as you demonstrate a brief retell for the students.

3. As readers demonstrate understanding, release responsibility so partners begin to work together as you mentor and coach. Remind students that the sketch should be brief (line drawing or stick figures), should utilize only one color, and should include labels.

4. Provide an opportunity for partners to share their sketches and their thinking. This helps students solidify their own understanding while giving them a chance to use the academic vocabulary and reprocess the information.

Extension: Once readers become proficient at using sketches and labels to represent their understanding of the content, invite them to write about the topic using the information from their sketch and labels.

Then, lead them in a discussion about how their sketches helped them as readers and writers.

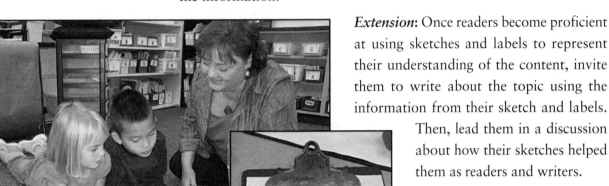

Visual representations support content retention and scaffold language use.

Reflection Questions for Sketch, Label, Share

How do my sketches and labels help me remember what I read?

How do my sketches and labels help me as I write?

When can I use this strategy during my school day?

Small Group

Partners

The Power of Questioning

Striving readers interact more meaningfully with informational text when they have an opportunity to ask questions *before*, *during*, and *after* reading. When these readers skim the table of contents, pictures, captions, and diagrams and ask questions, they are motivated to read with purpose because they are reading to answer their own ponderings. As more text is read and additional information absorbed, they can ask more questions and continue to look for answers to those questions. Finally, it's important for readers to understand that questions may linger long after the book is finished, leading them to look to other sources to answer their questions.

We know that student-generated questions strengthen comprehension, support content retention, and positively impact learning for striving readers (Keene and Zimmerman 2007; Duke and Pearson 2002; Allington 2009; Kendall and Khoun 2005). Therefore, it's important to show students how you ask questions before, during, and after reading. As you model your own wondering and reflection process, be sure to do so using a variety of texts from the instructional day. For example, as you read aloud from a book on Lewis and Clark in social studies, verbalize your own wonderings and encourage students to do the same. For this *solution*, take the time to expose striving readers to a variety of questioning styles as you model, so that they can see how questions and reflections can take many forms.

Following are some examples of questions and reflections that you can model before, during, and after reading.

Striving readers place questions on sticky notes as they read.

Steps for *The Power of Questioning*

1. Working with a small group of readers, present copies of a nonfiction text and invite students to work in pairs to skim the table of contents, photographs, headings, and diagrams to generate questions and ponderings.

2. Ask students to record their questions on sticky notes. Once they have had a chance to preview the text and ask questions, ask them to place their questions vertically on a large piece of paper.

3. Invite students to independently read the text and look for answers to the questions they have generated. Ask students to use another sticky note to record answers to their questions and place the answers next to the questions they asked during the preview of the text.

4. Invite students to record any *new* questions that surface as they are reading the text and place it in the Questions column of their paper.

5. Once students have finished reading the text, provide time for the group to discuss the process. *Were all of your questions answered? Do you have more questions now that you have finished reading? Where might we look for the answers to those questions?*

As readers become comfortable with the questioning process, invite them to work individually to record their wonderings as they read nonfiction texts independently.

Questions and answers are collected on a chart.

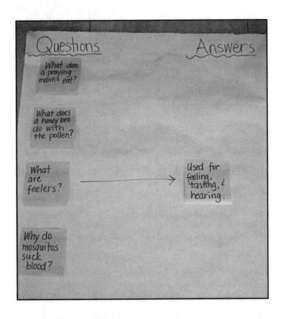

Questions and Reflections to Consider Before Reading	Questions and Reflections to Consider During Reading	Questions and Reflections to Consider After Reading
I wonder what this will be about?	I don't understand this. I wonder what the author is trying to say?	This book made me curious about _____. I wonder where I could find out more.
I have always been curious about _____. I wonder if the author will tell about it.	As I look at the picture on this page, I really wonder about _____.	The author didn't cover _____. Where can I find more information about that?
What a fascinating picture this is! I wonder if the author will tell me more about it.	What information does the author want me to remember from this page?	Which ideas were the most important to the author?
I really want to know about . . .	How do the photographs and captions help me on this page?	What was the author trying to say in this book?
I realize I don't know much about _____. I'm curious to know more.	Why did the author use this graph (or diagram, chart, cutaway)? What is important for me to remember?	What are the two or three most important things for me to remember from this book?
I once saw a program on TV about this. I wonder if this book will share similar information.	This part is so interesting to me! I wonder if the author will tell us more about it.	If I were to write a book on this topic, how would I organize it?

The Power of Questioning

Reader_____ Text_____ Date_____

Before reading, I wondered about

_____

_____

_____

_____

During reading, I wondered about

_____

_____

_____

_____

Now that I've finished reading, I still wonder

_____

_____

_____

_____

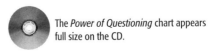

The *Questions and Reflections* chart appears full size on the CD.

The *Power of Questioning* chart appears full size on the CD.

Small Group

Partners

Jot It Down

Have you ever compiled a grocery list and then realized, upon arriving at the store, that you forgot the list at home? When this happens, many of us can (miraculously) remember most of the items on the list. This is because the *act* of writing the list actually helps the brain remember.

In this *solution*, we teach striving readers how to take meaningful notes while they are reading informational text—helping them learn a skill that can be used for the rest of their nonfiction reading lives. In fact, research suggests that providing opportunities for students to write about what they have learned in their reading supports content retention because it causes them to use the academic vocabulary immediately (Allington 2010; Marzano 2004; Pearson 2008).

Striving readers jot important words and phrases to solidify their understanding.

Steps for *Jot It Down*

1. Begin by using a picture or photograph from an enlarged text. Ask a small group of striving readers to look closely at the photograph and talk about what they can learn. Make a list of their words and phrases on index cards or large sticky notes.

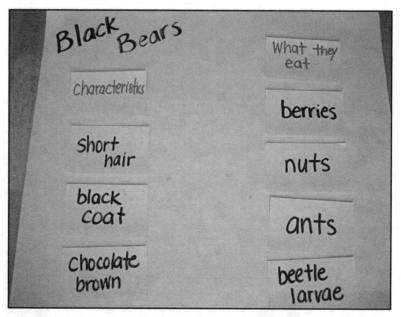

"Jot it" notes can be sorted and organized into meaningful categories to support summaries and retells.

2. Next, show students how you read a short section of the *text*, talk about the important ideas, and jot key words and phrases on sticky notes. Explain to students that the hardest part of taking notes about our learning is limiting the notes to just a few words.

3. As understanding of the process builds, invite students to join you in reading a short section and thinking about the words or phrases that would capsulate the learning.

4. Once you and your students have collected several notes, show students how you sort the sticky notes into categories that make sense. As the categories develop, students can place labels at the top of each category. The process of sorting the notes helps students realize that the purpose of notes is to gather similar ideas together so that, eventually, they can write about what they have learned in a way that is cohesive. (Sticky notes allow you to sort on a table top or on a piece of chart paper.)

5. As your striving readers seem ready, present partner pairs with copies of the book and invite them to continue reading and recording notes.

6. Coach and mentor readers as they sort notes and help them practice restating information orally to summarize their learning.

7. Provide time for the group to reflect on how taking notes and sorting them into categories helped them remember more about what they read.

OR

Whole Class   **Small Group**

Partners

Understanding Nonfiction Text Structure

Authors of nonfiction texts use a variety of internal text structures to organize the information they are presenting. When we teach striving readers how to use these structures to navigate informational text, comprehension and content retention soar!

In this *solution*, striving readers examine a specific text structure (sequential). Then, they use a graphic organizer to record information and use it to fuel a conversation about the text and its organization.

Steps for *Understanding Nonfiction Text Structure*

1. Select a book with a sequential text structure such as one focused on a life cycle (e.g., How a caterpillar becomes a butterfly).

2. On a chart, draw a graphic organizer that is linear and focused on sequence, such as this:

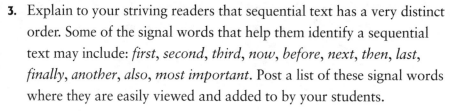

Students record signal words on an anchor chart about sequential texts.

3. Explain to your striving readers that sequential text has a very distinct order. Some of the signal words that help them identify a sequential text may include: *first, second, third, now, before, next, then, last, finally, another, also, most important.* Post a list of these signal words where they are easily viewed and added to by your students.

4. Begin reading aloud from the life cycle book you have selected, pausing each time you read a signal word to help the students notice the words as they appear in the selection.

5. Pause to do a brief retell of the steps in the life cycle so far, and add notes and sketches to the graphic organizer to reflect what has been read so far. As you retell, include temporal words such as *first, next, then, finally* in your oral summary.

6. When students appear to be ready, have them continue reading in partners and search for signal words. Coach and mentor by reminding them to pause frequently, retell, and then decide if they are ready to add sketches and words to their graphic organizer.

7. After reading, use the graphic organizer to support retelling as well as written summaries.

Understanding Nonfiction Text Structure also appears on the CD.

8. Over time, expose your striving readers to a variety of text structures and accompanying signal words as per the following text structure chart, creating an anchor chart with signal words and a graphic organizer for each text structure. Your striving readers will soon begin to recognize a variety of text structures and use those understandings to power up their comprehension.

The linear, time-order nature of sequential texts is well supported by a flow chart or linear story map.

Understanding Nonfiction Text Structure

Text Structure	Signal Words	Definition	Example
Cause and Effect	As a result, then, so that, because of, thus, unless, since, accordingly, consequently, reasons for, nevertheless, explanation for	The author explains the reasons for an event or episode. Cause is why something happened. Effect is what happened.	*Gray wolves were once in danger of becoming extinct because they were hunted illegally.*
Compare and Contrast	However, unless, although, while, in contrast, unlike, but, as well as, yet, on the other hand, either . . . or, compared to, similar to, same as, different from	The author shows how two or more things are alike and/or how they are different.	*Coyotes often hunt in pairs while wolves tend to hunt in packs.*
Time/Order or Chronological	First, second, third, now, before, next, then, last, finally, another, also, most important	The author describes items or events in order or tells the steps to follow to do something or make something.	*First, the wolf chases the prey toward a rendezvous point. Then, the other wolves who have been waiting there ambush the animal.*
Description	Is, have, look like, for example, involves, can be, defined, an example, for instance, in fact, also, contain, make up	The author describes a topic, idea, person, place, or thing by listing its features, characteristics, or examples.	*Gray wolves generally have gray, black, and light brown fur on their head and upper body.*
Problem/ Solution	The reason for, as a result of, because, a concern to consider, since, conclude, a solution is, a problem to resolve, how can	The author focuses on a problem and its solution.	*One problem to resolve in crocodile watching is transportation. How can an observer get close enough . . .*

Nonfiction Strategy Bookmarks

 OR

Whole Class   Small Group

Independent

Strategy Bookmarks appear full size on the CD.

Striving readers benefit from helpful tips and reminders that keep good reader strategies at the center of their thinking. Although anchor charts and posters are always helpful, this *solution* provides your striving readers with a personal bookmark that they can keep close at hand. For emergent readers, you may want to provide a prepared bookmark that includes small pictures to cue them. Developing and fluent readers may want to make their own bookmarks and feature the strategies that they are most currently addressing in reading.

You will find a variety of bookmarks on the following pages to use either as they are or as a springboard to bookmarks that you and your striving readers create together so they are personalized to their specific needs and your teaching points.

Steps for *Nonfiction Strategy Bookmarks*

1. Gather your striving readers close as you model reading from a nonfiction selection while referring to a copy of a Nonfiction Strategy Bookmark. Your think aloud might sound something like: *As I get ready to read, I am going to review the strategies on my bookmark. The first item is* Look at the pictures. *That is a good reminder. I don't want to start reading the words until I preview the pictures and think about the topic.* [After previewing pictures] *The photographs gave me some great ideas about the topic. I am ready to check the next strategy on my bookmark,* Ask questions. *I want to know about _____ and _____ and _____. Listen as I read these pages and see if my questions are answered.*

Bookmarks with nonfiction strategies can be personalized to the needs of each student.

2. Continue referring to the bookmark and modeling for readers.

3. Provide each reader with a Nonfiction Strategy Bookmark that matches their needs and your teaching points, plus a nonfiction book at their independent reading level.

4. As readers work independently, confer with individuals, assessing and coaching on their strategy use.

    Note: Be sure to notice that some of the example bookmarks that follow are personalized with pictures of readers. Kids love to have bookmarks that are personalized with their own image!

When I read nonfiction, I can:

 Look at pictures.

Ask questions.

 Stop often and think.

Look for labels.

 Make a picture in my mind.

Tell a friend what I am learning.

Strategies for Reading Nonfiction

- Look at the pictures.
- Look at the title.
- Examine headings.
- Look at captions and bold type.
- Make a picture in your mind.
- Predict: Make smart guesses.
- Think of "I Wonder" questions.
- Summarize in your head.
- Make sense!
- Chunk challenging words.
- Connect to what you know.
- Visualize.
- Reread!

My Book Checklist

Before reading, I
_____

____ Fiction

or

____ Nonfiction

____ Look at cover

____ Look through

____ Ask a **?**

I am ready to read!

Nonfiction Bookmark ✔

Before Reading, I

Look at the cover. ____

Look at the pictures. ____

Ask a question. ____

While I am reading, I

Stop and think. ____

Ask more questions. ____

Find important words. ____

After reading, I

share what I learned with a partner _____.

Reading Nonfiction

Previewing and Think . . .

What do I look for?

Text features I look for:
Titles, Headings, Bold words, Pictures, Captions, Maps, Charts, Graphs

Our Class Chart of Text Features . . .
I look for **BOLD** words.

I think how the words help me.

Reading Nonfiction

Previewing and Think . . .
What do I preview?
Text features I look for:
Titles, Headings, Bold words, Pictures, Captions, Maps, Charts, Graphs

Our Class Chart of Text Features . . .
I look for text features.

I tab them and think:
"This is important!" "It helps me . . ."

SOLUTION
to
Question
#2
NONFICTION

 OR

Whole Class   **Small Group**

Independent

Nonfiction Strategy Frame

For striving readers to take a metacognitive stance toward their behavior as a nonfiction reader, it is often helpful to create an anchor chart of strategies that good readers of informational text are likely to use. Each time you do a think-aloud and model a strategy that supports nonfiction reading, it can be added to the chart. Then, during small-group work or independent reading, you can mentor and coach your striving readers to utilize the cues on the chart as reminders to include these powerful strategies in their everyday reading. As confidence grows and striving readers need less cueing to activate these meaning-seeking strategies, they will enjoy filling out a Nonfiction Strategy Frame and celebrating their growing understanding of how to make the most of nonfiction passages. In this *solution*, readers use writing as a powerful tool for solidifying content understandings.

A Sample Anchor Chart

Good Readers of Informational Text

- Read for a purpose.
- Look over the text before reading to notice photographs, headings, charts, and so on.
- Use meaning—expect the text to make sense.
- Create visual images.
- Use text features such as captions, bold words, labels, arrows.
- Ask questions as they read.
- Reread to check details.
- Slow down when meaning isn't clear.
- Identify important words and ideas.
- Retell, summarize, and think about the content.
- Use a variety of fix-up strategies.
    - ✓ Read on.
    - ✓ Backtrack.
    - ✓ Use context clues.
    - ✓ Look at word parts: beginnings, endings, chunks.

Steps for *Nonfiction Strategy Frame*

1. Work with students over time to construct an anchor chart of Good Reader Strategies. Model and think aloud to be certain that striving readers understand how to apply each strategy.

2. Coach readers in these strategies during small-group instruction and personal conferences to move toward independence.

3. Revisit the anchor chart frequently and guide readers in a conversation about the strategies they think they are using effectively and which ones they still need to practice.

4. When striving readers have developed a good grasp of the strategies, invite them to complete a Nonfiction Strategy Frame as a way of highlighting and celebrating their progress as nonfiction readers.

5. Provide time for a discussion about the different responses they included in their strategy frame and send it home to celebrate with parents.

Nonfiction Strategy Frame also appears on the CD.

A Nonfiction Strategy Frame provides a structure to support striving readers as they reflect.

Nonfiction Strategy Frame

Reader_____ Date_____

As a reader of informational texts, I am learning that _____

_____.

When I am getting ready to read a nonfiction book, I take time to _____

_____.

During reading, I know it is important to _____

_____.

If I get stuck on a word, I _____

_____.

Strategies I use a lot in informational reading include_____

_____.

When I am finished reading about a subject, I _____

_____.

A goal for my next informational book is to _____

_____.

Informational books are different from stories because _____

_____.

  OR

Whole Class   **Small Group**

Partners

Text Features Scavenger Hunt

Informational texts have many unique features. These features are designed to support readers in navigating through resources and provide reader-friendly access to content. When striving readers expect these features to appear in informational passages, they can move in and out of the material with confidence and purpose. In this *solution*, the goal is to build this confidence and purpose with

When striving readers attend to and utilize text features, they gather more content.

text features—teaching nonfiction readers to notice and use these helpful features when they encounter them in text. They also need to utilize nonfiction text features when they produce nonfiction writing. When striving readers carefully note which features occur most often, what the features tell a reader, and which features help them most, they are empowered with tools that will help them gather more content and retain it.

To focus striving readers on text features in a manner that is interactive, physically active, and fun, you may want to try Text Feature Scavenger Hunts.

Steps for *Text Features Scavenger Hunt*

1. Work with striving readers to construct a list of text features that are most commonly found in the resources they encounter. (A list follows these steps for your reference.) It may be helpful to have a range of nonfiction selections close at hand so readers can investigate and add to the list.

2. Once the list is constructed, provide partner pairs with copies of the text features list they created or the one in this resource.

3. Model how to analyze a text and check for text features, then place tally marks on a text feature list. Your think aloud might sound something like: *I am searching this book for headings and I found fourteen! It is amazing that reading the headings gave me a really good idea of what this selection is going to be about. The headings help me think about main ideas so it would be easy to connect to the details when I read the entire passage.*

4. Provide partners with time to search a variety of books, counting features and tallying on their features lists. Most importantly, have them stop after each tally and consider how the text feature helps them as a nonfiction reader.

5. When the group gathers again, have partners report their findings. Which features appeared the most often? Were there any they did not find? Ask readers which features they should be especially careful to notice. Which features had the biggest impact on their comprehension? As writers, which features do they want to include in their writing?

Visual displays with examples of text features support striving readers as they learn to utilize these helpful nonfiction tools.

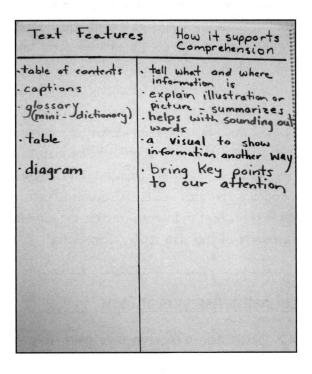

Nonfiction Text Features appears full size on the CD.

Nonfiction Text Features	
Communicate Information Visually	**Draw Attention to Important Ideas and Concepts**
Photograph	Title/headline
Illustration	Heading
Diagram	Subheading
Chart	Arrow
Graph	Boldface
Table	Caption
Flowchart	Table of contents
Storyboard	Glossary
Map	Index
Legend/key	Text box
Cross section	Bullet
Cutaway	Callout
Timeline	

What Written and Oral Responses Help Striving Learners Deepen Their Understanding of Nonfiction?

Side-by-Side Observation: Ali

Ali is learning English as an additional language. Her conversational English is established and she is currently receiving additional instruction focused on expanding academic language. During small-group instruction, Ali follows along with the group and attends to print during strategy instruction. However, when fellow students engage in partner or whole-group discussion, Ali slips into observer mode, becoming very quiet and hesitant to share. As we review our anecdotal notes as well as Ali's graphic organizers and written responses, we notice that both her writing and oral responses are limited to a small number of details. It is our belief that Ali needs to spend more time on a topic, exploring it through several reading selections to ensure vocabulary and concepts are in place. We decide to provide Ali with more scaffolds to support her oral and written responses to nonfiction, along with creating companion collections to support her reading.

Formative Assessment Tools

⇨ Observation of Oral Language, page 171

⇨ Individual Conference Notes, page 151

⇨ Reader Responses, page 185

Individual conferences provide essential opportunities for close observation of striving readers.

We Notice . . . In reflecting on our observations and formative assessments, we notice:

- Ali's conversational English is established, but she struggles with the academic language that is needed to sustain conversations about text.

- She is reluctant to engage in whole-group or partner discussions.

- Her oral and written responses are brief and do not represent a thorough understanding of what she is reading.

We Will Try . . . To help students like Ali participate comfortably in conversations and increase the quality of her written responses to informational text, we will try the following:

Stop, Share, Paraphrase
page 64

Small Group | Partners

Conversation Chips
on CD

Small Group | Partners

Conversation Stems
page 66

Whole Class | Small Group | Partners

Additional Solutions to Consider

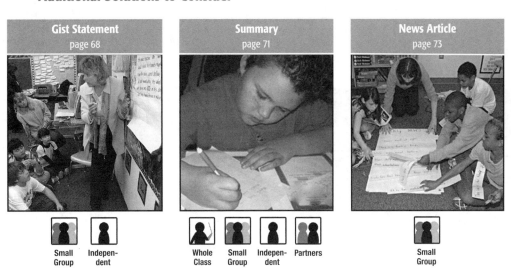

Gist Statement
page 68

Small Group | Independent

Summary
page 71

Whole Class | Small Group | Independent | Partners

News Article
page 73

Small Group

Small Group

Partners

Stop, Share, Paraphrase

Strong evidence suggests that oral language is the foundation on which reading comprehension is built and an essential learning focus for striving readers (Kletzien 2009; Cummins 2009; Gilliam and Carlile 2007). Stop, Share, Paraphrase is a scaffold that invites academic language use while helping striving readers gain access to pertinent content from their reading. In this *solution*, students work with a partner to read a small section of text, listen as their partner shares new learning from the text, and then paraphrase what is heard.

Steps for *Stop, Share, Paraphrase*

1. In advance of the session, identify points in a nonfiction text where it is natural to pause and share new learning. Mark these passages with a blank sticky note.

2. Invite a colleague, a teacher's assistant, or a student to act as your partner in a demonstration of the strategy. Decide in advance who will be Partner A and who will be Partner B.

3. Present a small group of readers with a chart outlining the steps: stop, share, paraphrase. (You may want to consider adding pictures or icons for each step to support emergent readers.)

Paraphrasing supports content retention and oral language proficiency.

4. With your partner, demonstrate how you read together until you reach the first sticky note in your book and then refer to the chart for the steps. First, *stop* and *share* something important that you have learned so far. Partner A shares first with a statement something like: *I learned that wolves typically hunt in packs of six to ten wolves and that they work together to kill large animals such as deer, elk, and moose.* Next, Partner B *paraphrases* what Partner A said with a statement such as: *I heard you say that wolves hunt in groups and that these groups can be as small as six or as large as ten. You also said that wolves hunt elk, moose, and deer.*

5. Continue to the next sticky note, reading together as your students observe. This time, Partner B is the first to share and Partner A paraphrases.

6. Continue for a few reciprocal turns. It may be helpful to model what to do when a partner is unclear about what was shared. In this case a question may be asked such as: *Please repeat that. Can you say that another way? Can you explain that to me?*

7. As understanding of the process builds, have students work in partner pairs and try the process in books that have preplaced sticky notes as stopping points. While partners try Stop, Share, Paraphrase, mentor and coach them in taking turns, sharing, and paraphrasing.

8. Provide an opportunity for partners to sum up and reflect on the new learning. Invite students to write one fact, idea, or concept that stood out from the text.

Question Stems for Stop, Share, Paraphrase
Can you please repeat that?
Can you say that another way?
Can you explain that to me?

 Note: A related solution, Conversation Chips, is available on the CD.

Whole Class OR **Small Group**

Partners

Conversation Stems for Nonfiction

One way to support striving readers as they engage in conversation is to provide Conversation Stems that can be used to encourage lively discussion. For this *solution*, we suggest that you and your students create an anchor chart of language stems that can keep a conversation going. Begin with a limited number of stems so your striving readers are not overwhelmed. As you and your students engage in more and deeper conversations about nonfiction, you can periodically add new stems so that discussions remain vibrant and engaging.

You'll want to be sure to post the chart in a place that will allow students to refer to it with ease. *Note*: See Part 2, page 124, for examples of conversation stems to support discussion when reading fiction.

Conversation Stems to Support Discussion appears full size on the CD.

Steps for *Conversation Stems for Nonfiction*

1. Present students with an anchor chart on which you have written a few Conversation Stems as provided on the next page. Invite a colleague, a teacher's assistant, or a student to act as your partner. Using

a familiar nonfiction book, demonstrate how you engage in a conversation using the stems listed on the chart to enrich your thinking. Each time one of you uses a stem from the chart, make a point to touch the stem so striving readers have a visual cue that you are not inventing the stems.

2. Invite the class to discuss how the chart helped the conversation reach a deeper level.

3. Invite partner pairs to talk about the stems and suggest additions to the chart.

Conversation Stems provide important support to striving readers as they enter conversations focused on nonfiction topics.

4. Provide ample opportunities for striving learners to take part in partner and small-group conversations using the stems to scaffold their discussions. Striving readers may need a personal version of the chart that they can keep close at hand to support their efforts to merge content and linguistic proficiency.

5. As your class engages in more and more discussions, revisit the chart to add stems or to delete stems that students do not find helpful.

TIP

The Conversation Stems can also support students as they write about their thinking. Consider inviting students to use the chart when asked to produce a written response to text.

Conversation Stems to Support Discussion

I learned . . .

I wonder . . .

I think . . .

One interesting thing I learned was . . .

I didn't know that . . .

I realized . . .

I think the author . . .

Now I understand how . . .

I find it interesting that . . .

I don't understand . . .

Do you think . . .

Why . . .

This is confusing because . . .

This part seems biased because . . .

I predict . . .

I think it means . . .

I get it now . . .

Why does the author . . .

What would happen if . . .

Do you agree that . . .

Now this is clear because . . .

I'm glad the author . . .

I'm picturing . . .

This is like . . .

The information here reminds me of . . .

I think the purpose of this book is . . .

If I were to write a book on this topic, I would . . .

If I could ask the author one question, it would be . . .

Start with a Gist Statement

Start with a Gist Statement offers striving nonfiction readers a framework that helps them present a summary that is focused on main ideas rather than a laundry list of details. Once striving readers learn the format, they produce smart-sounding summaries for oral responses to questions, interviews, or the short and extended responses required in many assessment tasks. The goal is to begin a summary with a gist statement that gives a big idea but no details. Then, a support is provided that proves the gist is true. Finally, a conclusion restates the gist and leaves a reader feeling confident that he has understood the main idea.

An Example

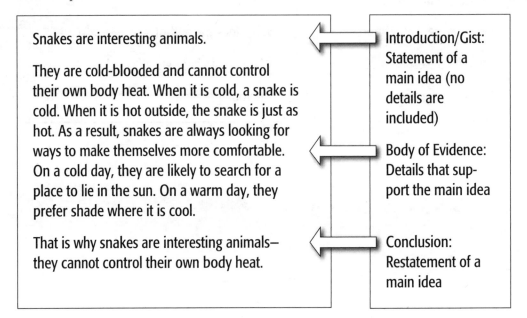

Snakes are interesting animals.

They are cold-blooded and cannot control their own body heat. When it is cold, a snake is cold. When it is hot outside, the snake is just as hot. As a result, snakes are always looking for ways to make themselves more comfortable. On a cold day, they are likely to search for a place to lie in the sun. On a warm day, they prefer shade where it is cool.

That is why snakes are interesting animals— they cannot control their own body heat.

Introduction/Gist: Statement of a main idea (no details are included)

Body of Evidence: Details that support the main idea

Conclusion: Restatement of a main idea

Steps for *Start with a Gist Statement*

1. Gather a small group to observe as you think aloud and model the construction of Start with a Gist Statement. Using a topic that is familiar to all group members, demonstrate how to create a gist statement that provides a big idea about the story but gives no details. The gist statement should leave a reader wondering "How?" or "Why?"

2. Write the gist on a chart as your striving readers observe.

3. Next, verbally list evidence or points of support for your gist statement. Identify details that "prove" your gist statement is true. Make a point to mention a detail of lesser importance and tell the readers why you are not including that detail.

4. Demonstrate how to create a conclusion that restates the introduction. Connecting words that may be helpful here include: *that is how, when, why, finally, in the end, to summarize.*

5. Mentor and coach as striving readers participate with you in the construction of a second Start with a Gist Statement. This could be about the same topic but focus on a different main idea. (For example, Snakes are legless eating machines.) Or, demonstrate with a new topic on a different day. The goal at this point is to have partners think together and contribute ideas for each section of the Start with a Gist Statement.

Framework for Start with a Gist Statement also appears on the CD.

6. As writers demonstrate understanding of the process, provide multiple opportunities to develop Start with a Gist Statement on a wide range of topics. Then move to independent application, as Start with a Gist Statement is a structure they can apply throughout their years in school.

A gist statement supports cohesive responses as it reminds a reader/writer of the main idea.

Framework for Start with a Gist Statement

Reader_____ Date_____

Topic_____

Make a sketch of something that is interesting or important about your topic.

Create a gist statement that introduces your information but provides no details. Tell what you are going to say. You want to make someone wonder *how* or *why*.

_____

_____

_____

Prove that your gist is true. What key points do you want to make?

-
-
-
-

Restate your gist. Conclude by reminding your listener or reader of your main idea. You may want to use words like: *that is how, when, why,* or *to summarize.*

 OR

Whole Class **Small Group**

Independent

Partners

Organizing a Summary

The ability to generate a summary orally and in writing is essential to everyday life and a survival skill for striving readers. The Organizing a Summary tool assists vulnerable learners in organizing their thoughts and preparing to generate an organized, cohesive summary. This *solution* begins with a labeled drawing to help striving readers integrate visual information and academic vocabulary. Then, learners are asked to share their labeled drawing with a partner as an oral rehearsal for the summary. During this oral sharing, readers are asked to share four key points about their topic. The sharing step is important as this is when striving readers rehearse their summary and elaborate on language.

Labeled drawings help striving readers focus on a central idea and utilize content-specific vocabulary.

A partner share with key points springboards striving readers into writing with confidence.

Organizing a Summary also appears on the CD.

Steps for *Organizing a Summary*

1. Using a book or topic that is familiar to both you and your students, demonstrate how to create a labeled drawing filled with details. As you create your drawing, show readers how you can draw lines between elements of the drawing and their corresponding labels so the connection is clear.

2. Next, think out loud and identify at least four key points you want to highlight about the information in your illustration. As students watch, create a bulleted list with key words and phrases that will help you remember the key points. Then, show readers how you double-check your drawing to ensure that all key points are represented in the visual.

3. Model a retell of the content, pointing to components of the illustration and ticking off each key point in your bulleted list as it is included in your retell.

4. Ask striving readers to talk with a partner about the process you used: a labeled drawing, bulleted list of key points, retelling of the content. Encourage them to offer opinions and suggestions.

5. Finally, gather your students close and model how to generate a written summary that includes the key points in your bulleted list and essential elements of your labeled drawing.

6. As striving readers express understanding of the process, provide opportunities for them to engage with Organizing a Summary independently as you mentor and coach.

Organizing a Summary

Reader_____ Title of Book_____

Topic_____ Date_____

Create an illustration that shows what you learned about this topic. Be sure to add labels to link important words and phrases to your drawing. You may want to add a caption, too.

```




```

Caption: _____

Plan a partner share. List key points you want to share with your partner below:

Tell your partner about your labeled drawing, making sure you include each of the key points you have listed:

(✓) I included this point when I shared my learning

- _____ (   )
- _____ (   )
- _____ (   )
- _____ (   )

Write about your topic. Be sure to include your key points and important information from your labeled drawing.

_____

_____

_____

_____

Small Group

News Article

News articles are a real-life text type that offers striving readers an opportunity to have their thinking published and shared in a very authentic format. To create a news article, students must identify key facts related to their topic, create connecting sentences, and organize the information in a way that is appealing to a reader. In first grade, the article may feature the life cycle of a frog, while fourth graders may generate an article on volcanoes or the civil rights movement. This kind of summarizing strategy is packed with important components such as determining important information, identifying the main idea(s), sentence combining, prioritizing ideas from least to most important, and synthesizing information. We feel this solution is a worthwhile investment as students summarize throughout their school years. As you can see in the images on these pages, News Article engages a group in actively constructing sentences on sentence strips then arranging them into a meaningful whole.

Striving readers generate statements of fact and arrange them in an order from most to least important.

Conversations about audience, connecting words and phrases, and clarity of content are a natural part of a news article experience.

March 17
Volume 1, Issue 1

Weekly News

This Week in Science: Owl Adaptations

Owls are birds of prey. These birds are nocturnal. They hunt food at night. Owls use their sharp talons to catch rodents. They use their sharp beaks to catch and eat food also. Their vision is ten times human vision. When owls fly their wide wingspan causes them to knock branches off of trees. These creatures have interesting features!

hoot

The finished article, ready to distribute to parents and other classrooms.

Steps for *News Article*

1. Read a newspaper article aloud, pointing out the emphasis on highly important information, rather than detail.

2. Have students create and organize sentences to hit the most important topics related to their subject.

3. Show them how to insert connecting words and phrases to ensure that the article reads smoothly and is pleasing to the ear when read aloud.

4. Type articles and assemble in a newspaper format.

Underlying Principles

- **Background knowledge,** also known as *schema*, is highly correlated to learning, understanding, and thinking. Readers think about what they already know in order to understand what they are reading (Pressley, Symons, Snyder, and Cariglia-Bull 1989; Cummins 2009; Dorn and Soffos 2005; Duke and Pearson 2002).

- **Comprehension and retaining content** is maximized when new information is embedded with personal experiences, interests, real-world connections, and realia (Willis 2007; Roller 1996; Schwartz 2006).

- **Student-generated questions** provide insight to what they know, wonder, and don't know. Their questions guide them to think, which leads to comprehension (Harvey and Daniels 2009; Keene and Zimmerman 2007; Hoyt 2009b; Fisher and Frey 2008).

- **Oral language** is the foundation on which reading is built. As children develop as readers, oral language continues to serve as the foundation of comprehension (Hiebert, Pearson, Taylor, Richardson, and Paris 1998; Britton 1992; Pearson 1999).

- **Forming mental images** and creating visual representations of text correlates highly to comprehension (Pearson 1999; Keene and Zimmerman 2007; Chard, Vaughn, and Tyler 2002).

- **Informational text** is loaded with specialized vocabulary, concepts, important ideas, and details (Hoyt 2002; Duke and Bennett-Armistead 2003).

- **Rereading** is more than a tool; it is a survival skill that helps readers uncover layers of meaning (Clay 2002; Routman 2002; Beers 2003).

- **Nonfiction text features** (titles, headings, captions, diagrams, boldfaced print, maps, graphs, bullets, flowcharts, photographs, labels, drawings, charts, and cutaways) signal importance and support comprehension (Harvey and Goudvis 2007; Stead and Hoyt 2011a).

- **Graphic organizers** offer visual support for internal text structure, supporting comprehension and content retention (Fountas and Pinnell 2006; Freeman and Freeman 2009; Jensen 2005; Klingner, Vaughn, and Boardman 2007).

PART TWO

Solutions for Comprehending Fiction

How Can I Help Striving Learners Understand and Effectively Summarize Fiction Selections?

How Can I Help Striving Learners Engage in Questioning and Inferring?

What Oral and Written Responses Help Striving Learners Deepen Understanding of Fiction?

PART 2

Solutions for Comprehending Fiction

*T*he comprehension of fiction is a highly active process requiring striving readers to weave an intricate network of information into a meaningful story line. To accomplish this, they must also attend to the problem–solution story structure, activate prior knowledge about people and culture, and make inferences about character motivation, setting, and possible solutions. They must also attend to situations that characters encounter and be sensitive to the ways in which the characters respond to challenges. Above all, striving readers must be *actively engaged* with the story line—taking a stance of reader responsibility, combined with conscious, reflective thinking.

Here are ten powerful factors for making fiction texts more accessible to striving readers.

1. Modeling and think-alouds: Although striving readers may be watching and listening during whole-class strategy demonstrations about how to comprehend a fiction selection, it is an unfortunate reality that the whole-class setting is not likely to offer adequate scaffolds for these vulnerable learners (Allington 2006). Evidence suggests that for striving readers to consciously apply comprehension strategies in fiction and nonfiction selections, they need to have additional teacher modeling and think-aloud experiences in small-group or one-to-one settings (Willis 2007; Harvey and Goudvis 2007; Cary 2007).

2. Conversations: When striving readers actively engage with thinking partners or small groups to have conversations about fiction, they have an opportunity to mediate understanding through supported dialogue and language use. The secret is to avoid hand raising and instead direct striving learners to consider questions with a partner. This sets the expectation that everyone needs to think, respond, and share—offering diversity of thought and enhanced comprehension (Schwarz 2006; Harvey and Daniels 2009; Hoyt 2007). Most importantly, this kind of distributed discourse boosts confidence and stimulates language expansion (Freeman and Freeman 2009).

3. Just-right books: Striving readers reach higher levels of comprehension when there is a just-right match between the reader and the text, the topic elicits strong personal connections, and the reader is drawn deeply into a story (Allington 2010; Echevarria, Vogt, and Short 2008; Klingner, Baughn, and Boardman 2007). When readers reach a state where they are *lost in a book*—compelled to read on to see what happens—active engagement at its deepest and most intrinsic level.

   In seeking just-right books, it is important that we—as coaches and mentors to striving readers—look at reading level but also consider familiarity of the content and linguistic patterns.

   ✓ If the setting and cultural perspective of the story are familiar to striving readers, they will find that comprehension is easier because their prior experiences will aid them in constructing meaning.

   ✓ Studies have shown that series books are particularly supportive of striving readers as the books present familiar characters and predictable story lines that can be visited again and again with each successive title (Krashen 2004).

   ✓ Lifelike characters, with behaviors like those of people in our lives, provide an advantage as well. When reading about lifelike characters, striving readers are more likely to see relationships between the characters in the story and people in their own world.

✓ Natural language patterns in the dialogue: For striving readers to reach maximum comprehension, the language patterns within dialogue should flow naturally so it sounds like oral language. The key is to ensure that the dialogue is not overly controlled or contrived (Echevarria, Vogt, and Short 2008; Roller 1996).

4. Visual representations: Visuals such as story maps, graphic organizers, storyboards, and sketches allow striving readers to reflect on a story through alternative systems of communication. The visual nature of these representations allows readers to "see" the relationship of ideas in pictures and spatial relationships rather than just in words (Pearson 2008; Vaughn, Gersten, and Chard 2000).

5. Explorations of story structure: Striving readers need to understand that fiction texts have a structure that is distinctly different than nonfiction sources. In fiction, Graves (1999) argues that *character* drives stories because stories are about what people want most and what they are willing to do to get it. This is helpful information for striving readers! If we can coach struggling students to pay close attention to what a character most wants and the steps he takes to get it, the plot will unfold naturally and make comprehension more accessible.

   Striving readers also need to expect that the character, or characters, operate within a certain setting, experiencing a series of events that focus on resolving a problem. The expectation that these elements are present will tune struggling students in as readers and thinkers, helping them to notice and attend to these features as they appear in the text. This fulfillment of expectation brings satisfaction and confidence to striving readers as they synthesize the pieces of information that make a work of fiction a meaningful story.

6. Retelling and summarizing: Retelling and summarizing have long been used as assessment tools, but they are also important scaffolds for enhancing fiction comprehension. Studies conducted with English language learners, special education students, and underachieving populations suggest that retelling builds understanding of story structure while facilitating oral language competence (Gilliam and Carlile 2007; de Quiros and Migdalia 2008; Dreher and Gray 2009; Howard 2010). In addition, PET scans indicate that the greatest brain activity occurred when readers were told they would be retelling or summarizing a story for someone else (Willis 2007).

> When striving learners use language as a tool for thinking and conversing, vocabulary development, English language proficiency, and content understanding are lifted simultaneously.

7. Questioning: When striving readers question a text and their own understanding of its meaning, they can be guided to reach beyond literal-level understandings and seek higher levels of comprehension. Questions are natural and one of the primary ways we learn about our world. Taking time to show striving readers how to ask questions before, during, and after reading can significantly impact their comprehension. As you coach students in generating and understanding questions, keep in mind that it is not necessary to begin conversations with literal questions. Sometimes the best comprehension is facilitated through aesthetic and critical/analytical responses that engage emotion or evaluative thinking (Pearson 2008; Keene et al. 2011; Kluth 2007; Cloud, Genesee, and Hamayan 2009; Raphael and Au 2005).

8. Physical action: Dramatic story reenactment and total physical response engage striving readers in using their physical self to represent essential elements of a story (Gill 2008; Tomlinson 2000; Klingner, Vaughn, and Boardman 2007; Freeman and Freeman 2009). Dramatization helps readers connect with character attributes, situations, mood, and tone.

9. Small-motor engagement: Even small movements help elevate engagement and increase reader interaction with a text. A simple yet helpful strategy is to have striving readers insert sticky notes into books as they identify points of significance. Sticky notes might be inserted when readers identify an important idea, wonder about and question the content, connect, visualize, infer, or find a portion of the story that they particularly enjoy (Hoyt 2009b; Kluth 2007; Tomlinson 2000; Vaughn and Linan-Thompson 2004).

10. Written responses: When the power of writing is combined with the power of analysis and reflection, striving readers are immersed in a language-learning atmosphere that is charged with possibility. Writing develops thinking and comprehension by creating a means for learners to reflect upon, modify, and extend their thinking about fiction (Hoyt 2009b; Common Core State Standards 2010). In addition, writing causes learners to call upon everything they know about reading—sounds, symbols, structures of language, and the construction of meaning all come together as a writer reflects and then writes about fiction texts (Short and Fitzsimmons 2007; Vaughn and Linan-Thompson 2004; Duke and Pearson 2002).

Fictional Text

If You Notice This:	*You Might Prompt This:*
⇨ **The reader gives an incomplete retelling of a story.**	• Tell me more. • What happened next? • What happened at the beginning, middle, and end? • Describe the setting. • What did you notice about the character(s)? • Tell about the problem and how it was solved.
⇨ **The reader does not connect to the story.**	• As you read, I am going to ask you to pause at the end of each page and say "I Wonder." Ask a question about the story. Think about what might happen next. Use questions to help yourself connect. • How are you like or different from the main character in this story? • Have you ever been in a similar situation? What did you think? Feel? Do? • What do you like or dislike about this story?
⇨ **The reader does not visualize.**	• Make a sketch showing the setting. • Describe a scene. • Describe the expression on the character's face when _____ happened. • If you were to draw a picture about this story, what would you include in your illustration?

continues

PROMPTS to Support Striving Learners

Fictional Text (cont.)

Prompts to Support Learning
Fictional Text also appears on the CD.

If You Notice This:	*You Might Prompt This:*
⇨ **The reader responds with details, not main ideas.**	• Tell me the three to five *most important* things that happened in the story. Why are they important? • Retell this story, focusing on the biggest and most important ideas. Be sure to include the problem and solution. • What do you think the author wants us to learn from this story? • Identify moments in this story that were memorable for you. Why were these moments important?
⇨ **The reader responds with literal interpretations of text.**	• If you could ask the author a question, what would it be? • If you were to rate this story on a scale of 1–10, what rating would you give it? Why? • Analyze this character. What is significant about the character's behavior? What motivates this character? • Are there any parts of this selection that you would change? • Select two words that reflect your thinking about this story. Tell why you chose those words.
⇨ **The reader sounds fluent but does not follow the story line.**	• Watch as I place sticky notes every few pages in your book. These are like stop signs. Each time you come to one, stop and think about what you just read. Then, make a little sketch or jot a word or two to help you remember what happened in this section. • As you read, it is important that you visualize the action and play a movie in your head. Read the next section and be ready to tell me about the picture you get in your mind.

QUESTION #1

How Can I Help Striving Learners Understand and Effectively Summarize Fiction Selections?

Side-by-Side Observation: James

A running record and a fluency assessment confirm that James is a child who reads with accuracy and fluency in grade-level material. However, when James is asked to respond to text through a retell or in writing, his responses to fiction reflect gaps in understanding. When asked questions about a text, James produces answers that are brief and underdeveloped. It appears that he is reading for speed and accuracy and that his understanding of the text is very shallow. It would be helpful for James to create pauses in his reading to facilitate active and conscious reflection on the story line. This would also reduce his concern for reading fast. He definitely needs to improve his understanding of story structure so his grasp of the plot improves. We believe it is important for James to have comprehension support through individual conferences as well as small group experiences.

Formative Assessment Tools

➪ Oral Reading Record, page 159

➪ Expressive Oral Reading Scoring Guide II, page 189

➪ Informal Retell Scoring Guide, page 179

➪ Fiction Retell Checklist, page 182

➪ Conferring Log: Comprehension, page 153

Sitting side by side presents a position of bonding and partnership.

We Notice . . . In reflecting on formative assessments, observations, and an interview with James, we notice:

- James takes pride in his ability to read accurately and quickly.

- His retell reflects gaps in understanding, whether the response is verbal or in writing.

- Although he is able to answer literal questions, he has trouble with inferential and critical/ analytical thinking.

We Will Try . . . To help James and others like him to read fiction with better understanding, we will begin with the following:

Predict–Check–Confirm
page 86

 Whole Class   Small Group   Partners   Independent

Character Wanted
page 93

Whole Class Small Group Partners Independent

Content Clues
page 95

 Whole Class Small Group Partners

Structured Summary
page 97

 A SMART JUICY AND

 Whole Class Small Group One-to-One Partners

Additional Solutions to Consider

Beginning, End . . . Middle
page 88

Small Group Partners Independent

Story Mapping
page 90

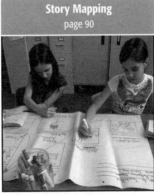

  Whole Class Small Group Partners Independent

Five-Finger Retell
page 100

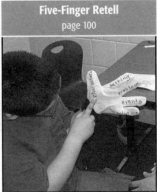

  Whole Class Small Group Independent

Very Important Points
page 101

   Whole Class Small Group Partners Independent

Key Words
page 102

    Whole Class Small Group Partners Independent

 OR

Whole Class **Small Group**

Partners

Independent

Predict–Check–Confirm or Revise

Striving readers, like James, engage more fully with fiction selections when they take time to make a prediction, then read to see if their prediction is confirmed within the story. When we coach striving readers to predict, read, and then predict again, intrinsic motivation is inherent because they are reading to see if their own prediction turns out to be supported by the text. This interactive process raises engagement and helps striving readers understand that comprehension evolves as they move through a text. As more text is consumed and additional information added, striving readers search for evidence that a prediction has been confirmed. If the text does not support the prediction, then the reader must take responsibility to modify and adjust understanding. Being "right" is not the goal, but rather to know that predictions are reasonable based on clues within the story.

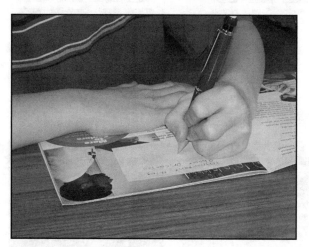

A reader records predictions on sticky notes during small-group instruction.

As you engage with this *solution*, be sure to model your own predictive processing for striving readers—with a whole class or small group—with a selection that is new to you so that your predictions are genuine and your think-aloud is as authentic as possible. The authenticity of your reaction to incoming information will guide you in thinking aloud and give you an opportunity to show genuine surprise or interest regarding clues you might have missed if the author surprises you.

An example: *I predict the preacher will let Opal keep the dog, Winn-Dixie, because that's the way realistic fiction works. Winn-Dixie is in the title of the book and that means Winn-Dixie will probably be a major character throughout the book. It wouldn't be much of a story if the main character isn't present. Opal is lonely and the preacher knows that she desperately needs a friend and companion. So far in the story the preacher seems to have a big heart and I predict it would be in keeping with his character to let Opal keep the dog* (Because of Winn-Dixie *by Kate DiCamillo).*

Steps for *Predict–Check–Confirm or Revise*

1. In advance of the lesson, identify points in a story where it is natural to pause and make predictions. Mark these passages with a sticky note.

2. Present students with a chart displaying the steps: Predict—Check—Confirm or Revise. You may want to add icons to assist emergent readers.

3. Model how you read until you get to the first sticky note in your book and pause to predict. Then, tell the students to listen closely as you read on to *check* to see if your prediction is confirmed by the story or if the prediction needs to be revised. While reading, pause often and think aloud: *Has the prediction been confirmed by the story or do I need to revise my thinking?* Be sure to think aloud at points where a prediction is confirmed, and help striving readers notice when a prediction needs to be revised.

4. As understanding of the process builds, invite students to turn to a partner and make predictions. Then after reading on for a bit, have partners decide if the prediction has been confirmed or needs to be revised.

5. To further deepen understanding, gather a group of three to five students or an individual for a reading conference. Then, present striving readers with a text you have prepared with preplaced sticky notes as stop points for prediction. Have readers stop at each sticky note and Predict—Check—Confirm or Revise, stating their prediction of what will happen next and why. This encourages thoughtful reasoning, rather than wild guessing.

6. Provide an opportunity for partners to reflect on their predictions, considering those that were confirmed and those that needed revision.

7. As readers mature in their understanding of the strategy, they may benefit from taking time to write predictions on sticky notes within the book as they read independently.

Small Group

Partners

Independent

Beginning and End . . . Then the Middle

Although it is important for striving readers to think about the progression of events in a story, they can easily become bogged down in the "middle" and lose track of the ending. To scaffold their understanding of overall story structure, this *solution* coaches striving readers to focus first on the beginning and the end, then go back to the middle. Once the beginning and end are established, these elements serve as bookends, making it easier for striving readers to consider the middle portion of the story in terms of main ideas.

Steps for *Beginning and End . . . Then the Middle*

1. Create a chart labeled Beginning, Middle, End.

Beginning	Middle	End

2. In a small group setting, present a familiar text and think aloud to identify the initiating event, or beginning, of the story. On the chart, record in pictures and/or words a description of the beginning. Example: *Goldilocks went into the house of the bears even though they weren't at home.*

3. Next, focus your attention on the end of the story, thinking aloud about the end and how you know when a story is complete. Model how to use pictures and/or words to create a description of the concluding event, the end, on the chart. Example: *Goldilocks woke up when the bears came home and raced back to her own house as fast as she could.*

Sketches assist striving readers in keep track of Beginning, End . . . Then Middle.

4. Finally, think aloud about the events that occurred in the middle of the story. Explain that to describe the middle of a story, it is most helpful to think about the main ideas that hold the story together. Example: *A main idea is that Goldilocks acted like she could do whatever she wanted in the bears' house. She ate the porridge, sat on the chairs, and tried all the beds. Main ideas are a helpful way to explain the middle of the story.*

5. Over time, continue to mentor and guide striving readers as they identify the Beginning and End . . . Then the Middle of stories they read with small-group support or independently. Provide time for partners to discuss their thinking and share the charts they create.

6. As striving readers develop confidence with the strategy, they may enjoy recording sketches and notes for the beginning, end, and middle on sticky notes as they read independently.

A reader writes about Beginning, End . . . Then Middle on sticky notes.

 OR

Whole Class   **Small Group**

Partners

Independent

Story Mapping

Story maps provide a structure to help striving readers visually present their understandings about a story. Although there are a variety of story map frameworks available, most include the basic story grammar of characters, setting, problem, events, and solution. To best support striving readers, be sure to choose an organizational structure

Story maps offer a visual support system that is highly supportive of striving readers.

that matches the story line of your text. For example, if you are reading *If You Give a Mouse a Cookie* by Laura Numeroff, be aware that its circular structure would not be a good match to most story maps. This book would be better matched to a flowchart or storyboard with arrows showing the cause-and-effect relationship in each event. (See the Cause-and-Effect Organizer on page 91.)

Pink and Say by Patricia Pollacco, in comparison, has a straightforward problem-and-solution structure that is perfect for maps such as those provided here. In this *solution*, you will want to select a story map that matches the organizational structure of the reading material you will be using with your striving readers.

Steps for *Story Mapping*

1. Choose a story with a clear structure.

2. Select a story map framework that matches the story's structure.

3. Model your thinking as you complete a story map, demonstrating the process with a story familiar to the students.

4. Have the students complete story maps in pairs or within a small group using a text that is familiar to all participants.

5. As readers gain confidence, have them complete story maps for selections they have read independently.

6. Use completed story maps as a scaffold for partner discussion or springboards to writing well-organized summaries.

The *Story Maps* appear full size on the CD.

Story Map

Characters:	Setting:	Problem:
Event:	Event:	Solution:

Story Map

Setting:
Characters:
Event:
Event:
Event:
Solution:
Theme or lesson:

Main Idea

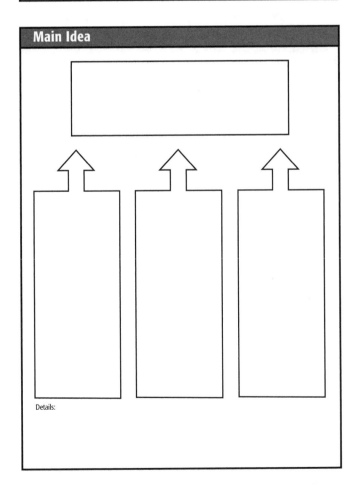

Details:

For a Circular or Cause-and-Effect Structure

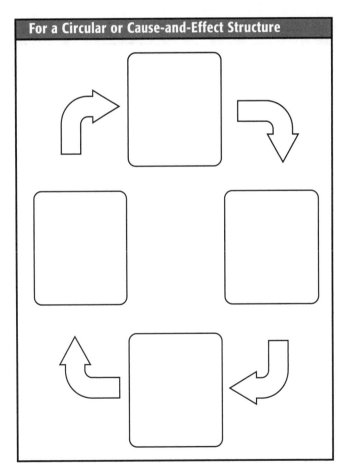

Storyboard

Reader_____ Book_____

Write or draw to show story events in the order they happen in your book.

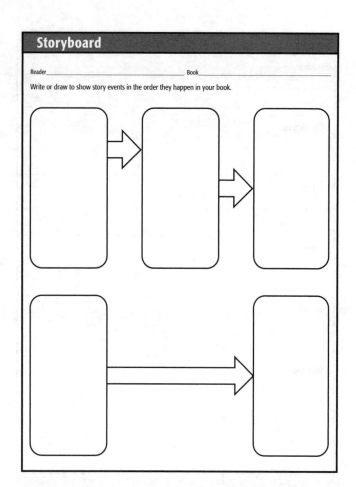

Story Map

Title: _____

Author: _____

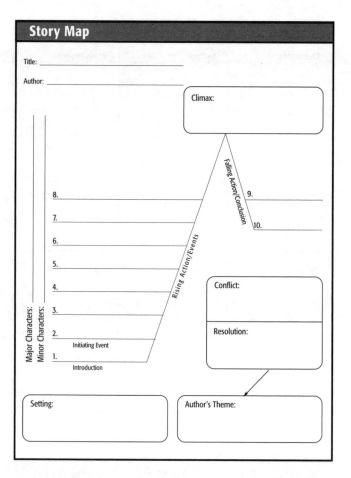

Climax:

Falling Action/Conclusion

Rising Action/Events

8. _____   9. _____
7. _____   10. _____
6. _____
5. _____
4. _____   Conflict:
3. _____
2. _____
Initiating Event   Resolution:
1. _____
Introduction

Major Characters:
Minor Characters:

Setting:

Author's Theme:

Genre Map

Genre: _____

• Distinguishing Features:
_____
_____
_____

• Example of Genre:
_____
_____

Genre: _____

• Distinguishing Features:
_____
_____
_____

• Example of Genre:
_____
_____

Fiction
Genres

Genre: _____

• Distinguishing Features:
_____
_____
_____

• Example of Genre:
_____
_____

Genre: _____

• Distinguishing Features:
_____
_____
_____

• Example of Genre:
_____
_____

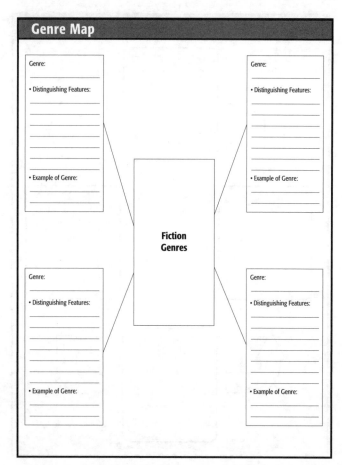

Cause/Effect Organization

Signal Words for Cause/Effect:

because, since, if/then, due to, as a result, for this reason, on account of, consequently

Cause	Effect
The pilot in Hatchet collapsed against the wheel of the airplane.	As a result, Brian had to try to land the airplane.
Cause	Effect
Cause	Effect

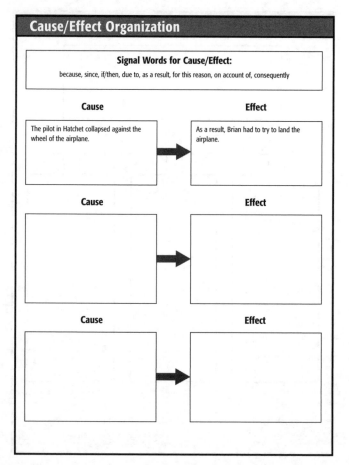

Whole Class OR **Small Group**

Partners

Independent

A Character…Wanted… But…So… and *A Character…Wanted… But…So…Then…* appear full-size on the CD.

A Character Wanted

(adapted from Macon, Bewell, and Vogt 2002)

A Character Wanted is a scaffold that supports striving readers in understanding the progression of plot and the way that character motivation affects the storyline. In addition, this *solution* empowers striving readers with a language frame and connectives (*but*, *so*, and *then*) that support language expansion and effective sentence construction.

A Character Wanted can also be used to support point of view by completing the chart for oppositional characters. For example, you might complete one chart from Little Red Riding Hood's perspective and then do an additional chart showing the perspective of the wolf. Examples follow:

Little Red Riding Hood			
A Character	**Wanted** (Goal or Motivation)	**But** (Problem or Conflict)	**So** (Solution/Resolution)
Little Red Riding Hood	wanted to take goodies to Grandma.	But the wolf was in the way.	So she went a different way.

Stone Fox by John Reynolds Gardiner			
A Character	**Wanted** (Goal or Motivation)	**But** (Problem or Conflict)	**So** (Solution/Resolution)
Grandpa	needed money to take care of Little Willy and run the farm.	But he was too sick to get out of bed.	So, Little Willy and Searchlight harvested the potatoes and entered the dog race.

You can extend the sophistication of this technique for more competent readers by adding a fifth column, *Then*, to focus on climax or falling action.

Little Red Riding Hood				
A Character	**Wanted** (Goal or Motivation)	**But** (Problem or Conflict)	**So** (Solution/Resolution)	**Then** (Climax)
Little Red Riding Hood	Wanted to take goodies to Grandma.	But the wolf was in the way.	So, she went a different way.	Then, the wolf was waiting at Grandma's house and Little Red Riding Hood was saved by the hunter.

Once striving readers catch onto the gist of the process, the key words *a character*, *wanted*, *but*, *so*, and *then* can be used to support a retell or summary as per the following example for *Shiloh*.

Students make flip charts with sketches on the front and writing inside to retell a story using the A Character Wanted strategy.

Shiloh by Phyllis Reynolds Naylor

Marty wanted *a dog* but *he knew that his family couldn't afford one*, so *when he found Shiloh he hid him*. Then Marty wanted *to get food for Shiloh but he didn't have any money*, so *he collected cans to raise money*. Then Marty wanted *to keep Shiloh safe* but *the big black dog jumped the fence and attacked Shiloh*, so *Shiloh was badly injured*. Then . . .

Steps for *A Character Wanted*

1. In a whole-class or small-group setting, create a four-column chart as per the earlier examples and guide striving readers in a conversation about what a character *wanted* in a familiar story. As the students observe, fill out column 1 on the chart using both sketches and words. This adds a layer of visual support that can be very helpful to striving readers.

2. Model how to use the key word *but* to talk about and then record obstacles that were in the way of the character achieving a goal.

3. Then, discuss how the character resolved the dilemma and record that information in the fourth column.

4. Provide guided practice by having partners work together to complete A Character Wanted chart about a familiar story and then present it to another partner pair.

5. Over time, build independence by having striving readers complete a chart alone before sharing with a partner.

 OR

Whole Class   **Small Group**

Partners

Content Clues

Content Clues is a *solution* that provides three important levels of understanding for striving readers: content clues taken directly from the text, main idea statements, and an evaluative statement of opinion. The content clues are preselected by the teacher and presented to students as a list. These clues represent important ideas (phrases and words) that are essential to a high-quality summary. After reading, students work in partner pairs to review the content clues and prepare to retell the content using the clues. Next, the teacher and the students work together to create main idea statements that link details and events. Finally, students generate evaluative statements of opinion in which they assess, judge, evaluate, and consider quality. This multifaceted system of support helps striving readers produce retells and summaries that are strongly tied to the plot, while also inviting them to address the text with an analytical stance.

Content Clues for Goldilocks and the Three Bears
• soup
• chairs
• bed
• discovery
Main Idea: Goldilocks broke into the home of the bears, even though she knew better.
Opinion Statement: Goldilocks needs to apologize and clean up the mess.

Steps for *Content Clues*

1. First, demonstrate how to use a list of content clues to generate a retell or summary of a text that is familiar to your striving readers. As you model infusing these clues into a retell, it will help to show readers how you return to the text—rereading and confirming your facts.

2. Next, show students how to create a main idea statement that links all the clues. An example: *Goldilocks treated the home of bears as though it was her own—until the bears found her.*

3. Finally, model how to offer an opinion about the selection overall. What did you think of Goldilocks' behavior? What rating would you give it if this were a book review? What is your assessment of the quality of the writing? And so on. Example: *I think Goldilocks was very naughty. She should have to go back and apologize to the bears, then clean up the mess she made.*

4. When students appear to understand the process, provide content clues (words and phrases) from a new selection that is comfortable reading for partners. Have partners think together to be sure they understand each clue, returning to the text to reread and confirm as needed.

5. Partners use the clues to generate an oral retell or a summary.

6. Students work as a team to create a main idea statement or two, discussing which clues fit with which main idea statements.

7. Partners generate an evaluative opinion statement.

An Example for *Snowflake Bentley* (a nonfiction narrative)

1. Students use teacher-provided content clues (words and phrases) to generate a retell or summary.

Content Clues
• Focused on snowflakes
• Studied patterns of flakes
• Photographer
• Scientist
• Lifelong learner
Other words and phrases that are important to remember

2. The students and teacher create a main idea statement or two based on the content clues:

   • Snowflake Bentley devoted his life to the study of snowflakes.

   • He became an expert photographer and provided important information on the science of snowflake patterns.

3. Coach partners to generate an opinion about the selection: *The organization of the book is really interesting. There is a story running under the illustrations and then facts along the sides that really add a lot of detail. The author was very creative.*

Content Clues is adapted from the work of Linda Gambrell.

Structured Summary

A Structured Summary offers striving readers a framework that helps them present a summary that is focused on main ideas rather than a laundry list of details. This is of enormous importance as we have all seen how vulnerable readers can gather morsels of literal information but struggle to integrate the pieces into a big idea (Walmsley 2006). Once striving readers learn the format, they can apply the structure to many different situations including oral responses to questions, interviews, or the short and extended responses required in many assessment tasks. A Structured Summary has the following components: introduction, body of evidence, and conclusion.

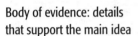

Whole Class   OR   **Small Group**

One-to-One

Partners

Introduction: statement of a main idea (no details are included)

Body of evidence: details that support the main idea

Conclusion: restatement of a main idea

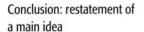

Fiction Example

The Three Little Pigs were harassed by the wolf but they won in the end.

In the beginning, the wolf huffed and puffed, blowing down the house of straw and the house of sticks. Then, he tried to blow down the house of bricks and even tried to climb down the chimney. But finally, the pigs outsmarted him by having a fire burning in the fireplace.

The big bad wolf gave it his best shot but the house of bricks and a small fire turned the tide for the pigs. The wolf limped away with a singed tail and a wounded ego.

Modeling provides concrete support as striving readers learn how to write structured summaries.

Steps for *Structured Summary*

1. Gather the whole class or a small group to observe as you think aloud and model the construction of a Structured Summary. Using a story that is familiar to all group members, demonstrate how to create an introduction that provides a big idea about the story but gives no details. The introduction should leave a reader wondering "But how?" or "What happened?"

2. Write the introduction on a chart.

3. Next, verbally list evidence or points of support for your introduction. Identify details that "prove" your introduction is true.

4. Add the details to the summary in sentence format, using connecting words such as *to begin with*, *in the beginning*, *most importantly*, and so on.

5. Demonstrate how to create a conclusion that restates the introduction. Connecting words that may be helpful here include: *that is how, when, why, finally, in the end, to summarize.*

6. Mentor and coach as striving readers participate with you in the construction of a second Structured Summary. This could be about the same story but focus on a different main idea. (For example: *The first two pigs weren't very smart.* Or, use a new story on a different day. The goal at this point is to have partners think together and contribute ideas for each section of the Structured Summary.

7. As writers demonstrate understanding of the process, provide multiple opportunities to develop structured summaries on a wide range of stories and topics as they read and write independently.

Fourth- and fifth-grade students worked collaboratively to construct Structured Summaries in Yvonne Hays classroom in Hudson, Ohio.

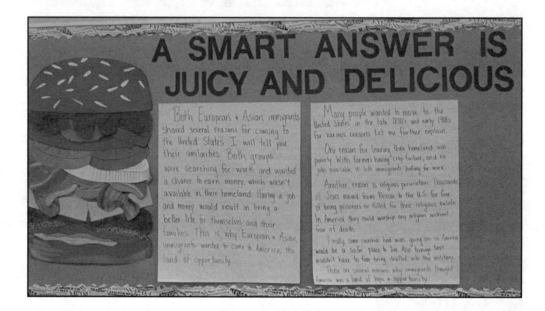

Structured Summaries enable striving readers to write well-organized, thoughtful summaries.

The poem Country Grandmother by Brad Bagert is a Hilarious and exciting poem about a funny grandmother.

At the beginning, the poem talks about what you would think the kids' grandmother is like. Then it talks about How she really is. She is not like the other grandmas. Here are some things she does. She jogs. She reads, she mows her own two-acre of lawn and she attends college classes. The poem ends when she says no matter what happens she will always plan to have fun.

We liked the poem because it was funny and it reminded us about our grandmas. She is Humorous, adventurous, and exciting to be around, just like our grandmas!

Summary by:
Michaela Saing
Hayden Feathers
Max Katila
Meghan Brunching

Identify a main character in your novel and describe characteristics of this character. Support your ideas with details from the text.

In the book *Brian's Winter* the main character is Brian. I will describe 3 characteristics about Brian.

First, I think he was grateful. In the story Brian was grateful about all the food he had. The part that described it was when the passage said, " He tried to ration the food out but found it impossible, and within two weeks he had eaten it all, even the package of dried prunes- something he had hated in his old life." He was thankful to have any kind of food to stay alive.

Secondly, I thought he was foolish. In the story Brian was foolish when he kicked a bear's rear end when the bear came walking into his shelter. The story said, " Brian pulled back a foot. Hey get out of here! He yelled, and kicked the bear in the rear." Even though Brian was brave to do this, the bear could have killed him!

Finally, I thought he was intelligent in coming up with ways to survive. He was intelligent when he thought of making arrowheads to hunt with. The part that described it was when the passage said, "Flint. There the word came to him. They weren't just arrowheads, they were flint arrowheads- maybe they had to be flint to chip right." Another example of smart survival is not wasting parts of animals that he hunts and kills. "The head, and lungs and intestines and stomach and liver he set aside for fish bait and food, as well as the heart."

Those are 3 characteristics about Brian. I hope you learned more about Brian and some traits to help him survive in the Canadian wilderness.

By: Nate Hensel
Mrs. Hays' Class

Structured Summary Checklist

1. Did you open with an introduction (main idea or a gist) that provides no details and makes a reader wonder?

2. Did you fill the middle section with evidence to support your main idea?

3. Did you use connecting words so the sentences flowed together smoothly?

4. Did you restate the main idea in the conclusion?

5. What are the strengths of your Structured Summary? What did you do particularly well?

Extension idea:

This solution is highly transferable and easily used with informational topics as well.

Nonfiction Example

It is important for everyone to recycle because recycling conserves natural resources and protects the earth.

For instance, paper is made from trees, and if we recycle paper there are more trees available to prevent erosion, produce oxygen, and clean the air. In addition, there is evidence that plastic sent to landfills or thrown in the ocean is making sea creatures ill and increasing the greenhouse gases produced in landfills. Similarly, metals can easily be melted, reused, and reshaped so their usefulness continues without taking more minerals from the earth.

To summarize, it is important for everyone—each person on the planet—to recycle because recycling conserves resources and protects the earth.

 OR

Whole Class   **Small Group**

Independent

Five-Finger Retell

Five-Finger Retell is a *solution* that can support striving readers in delivering a more comprehensive retell or summary. The objective is to utilize visual cues in combination with small-motor movements as students touch each of their fingers and identify a story element (problem, solution, characters, setting, events) for each one. Striving readers who need explicit visual support may benefit from tracing around their hand and then labeling each finger in their drawing with a literary element. As students demonstrate readiness to add theme or author message to their retells, a heart labeled with the word *theme* or *author's message* can be added to the palm of the hand.

In *Revisit, Reflect, Retell* (2009b), Linda Hoyt writes about using a plain white garden glove and writing story elements on the fingers of a Storytelling Glove. Striving readers love to slip into a glove and retell the story elements as they touch each finger, or pause to reflect and share the "heart," which is the author's message.

A student proudly displays a Five-Finger Retell glove.

Steps for *Five-Finger Retell*

1. Display a plain, white garden glove that has been labeled with the elements of story structure needed in a quality summary or retell.

2. Choose a book that has a well-defined structure: characters, setting, problem, events, and solution. Read it to the students or guide them in a reading experience.

3. Think aloud and demonstrate how you touch each finger (structural element) on the glove to remind yourself of the elements that must be in place for a quality retell. Present a complete retell so your striving readers see and hear what is expected.

4. Have students use the Five-Finger Retell procedure to retell stories in pairs or in small groups.

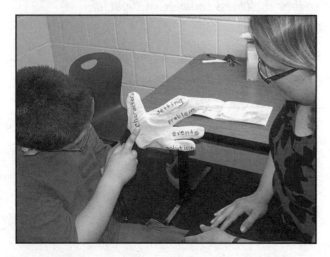

A Retelling Glove helps striving readers to remember essential structural elements of a story.

 OR

Whole Class **Small Group**

Partners

Independent

Very Important Points (VIPs)

The VIPs Strategy (Hoyt 2009b; Stead and Hoyt 2011a) engages striving readers in using sticky notes cut into slim strips to mark important points in their reading. With teacher guidance, this *solution* directs striving readers to flag key points and ideas that are interesting or confusing or a place where they have a personal connection. Based on current areas of instruction, they might flag an inference, a place where they had a question, or a passage that helped them visualize. Following the reading, partners compare VIPs and tell why they selected each point. The follow-up conversation is vital. It gives readers a chance to compare observations and defend their thinking, using language and shared dialogue as tools for understanding.

Steps for *VIPs*

1. In a whole-class or small-group setting, model how to determine importance while reading, and then mark a passage that you identify as being *very* important. An enlarged text, a document camera, or overhead projector can make this process highly visible for striving readers.

2. Provide students with sticky notes and show them how to cut strips so that each strip has a bit of sticky material on it.

3. Have students insert VIPs into the text as they read to mark important points in the text.

4. Invite readers to share their VIPs with a partner or in a small group, emphasizing that they need to tell *why* they chose each VIP.

5. As readers gain confidence, you can add an evaluative element by having them choose the five most important VIPs to support a summary of the story.

VIP points focus attention and help striving students identify key points in a work of fiction.

Whole Class   OR   **Small Group**

Partners

Independent

Key Words to Summarize

To summarize, striving readers must identify the most important parts of a story and then create a synthesis of those parts. The summary must be succinct and reflect the gist of the story with only the most significant details included. It is likely that striving students will need multiple demonstrations with modeling and guided practice before using this strategy independently, but it will be worth the effort.

Steps for *Key Words to Summarize*

1. In a whole-class or small-group setting, model how to read a portion of a text and then think aloud about key words and phrases that might be saved to use in a summary. Show the students how to select and record an important word or a very short phrase on a sticky note, then continue reading. Place only one key word or phrase per sticky note.

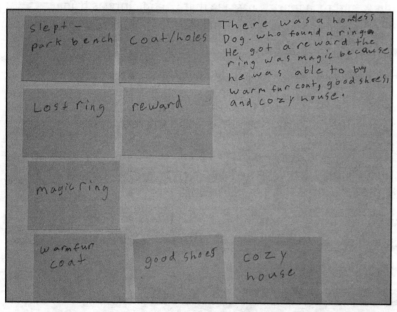

Key words and phrases support comprehension and power up summaries.

2. After a number of key words and phrases have been identified, pause and think aloud as you arrange the sticky notes in an order that supports a summary. Continue modeling and thinking aloud to demonstrate how to collect words and summarize.

3. Have partners select words and very short phrases from a story that they believe are important to their understanding of the selection. Ask them to write those words on individual sticky notes.

4. After reading, have partners close their books and use the sticky notes to generate an oral or written summary.

5. Once readers become proficient at picking out literal-level key words, they may benefit from focusing on key words that infer something about the text. For example, key words might be selected that reflect the mood of the story, character traits, levels of tension, themes, lessons, and so on.

6. Over time, readers will find that this strategy can be used independently, too.

(Originally, presented in Hoyt, *Make It Real*, 2002.)

Key Word Strategy also appears on the CD.

Key Word Strategy

Reader_____ Date_____ Book Title_____

Key Words:

Summary:

_____

_____

_____

_____

_____

_____

How Can I Help Striving Learners Engage in Questioning and Inferring?

Side-by-Side Observation: Ruby

Ruby reads accurately, at a pace that is appropriate to the text, and adjusts phrasing in response to meaning. In addition, Ruby retells story events in sequential order. However, Ruby does not show evidence of understanding how to infer, generate questions as she reads, or make personal connections to the text. To ensure that this wasn't a single event caused by a mismatch between Ruby and the text, we confer with her several times and utilize a Conferring Log for Comprehension (see page 153) to gather formative data. As suspected, ongoing data confirm that Ruby needs explicit support in reaching for deeper comprehension. We plan to provide think-alouds and demonstrations in small-group and one-to-one settings, provide structured reader response opportunities, and involve her in experiences focused on questioning and inferring.

Formative Assessment Tools

⇨ Conferring Log for Comprehension, page 153

⇨ Expressive Oral Reading: Multiple Observations, page 190

⇨ Strategy Scoring Guide, page 155

⇨ Informal Retell Scoring Guide, page 179

Close observation provides important insights into the strategies being used by striving readers.

We Notice . . . In reflecting on observations and conferences with Ruby, we notice:

- Ruby is a fluent and accurate reader.

- She can retell stories with accuracy and in sequential order.

- In discussions and written responses, her contributions are surface-level.

- There is little evidence of personal connections, self-questioning, or inferential thinking.

We Will Try . . . To help Ruby, and readers like her, dig deeper into fiction selections, we will begin with the following *strategies*:

I Can Infer
page 106

 Whole Class   Small Group   Partners   Independent

Two-Word Strategy
page 108

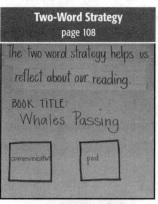

The two word strategy helps us reflect about our reading.

BOOK TITLE:
Whales Passing

communication   pod

 Whole Class   Small Group   Partners

Question Generating
page 111

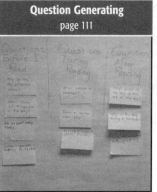

 Whole Class   Small Group   Partners   Independent

Quality Questions
page 113

Small Group   Partners   Independent

Additional Solutions to Consider

Inference Equation
page 110

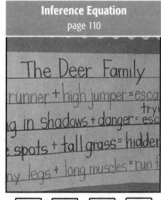

The Deer Family
runner + high jumper = esca
                          try
g in shadows + danger = esc
e spots + tall grass = hidden
ny legs + long muscles = run f

 Whole Class   Small Group   Partners   Independent

I Wonder
page 116

 Whole Class   Small Group   Partners   Independent

Connect to Fiction
page 118

 Whole Class   Small Group   Partners

Question-Answer Relationships
page 119

 Whole Class   Small Group   Partners   Independent

I Can Infer

To set the stage for conscious inferences, this *solution* focuses striving readers on how inference is created when clues are combined with prior knowledge. For example, seeing dark clouds in the sky is a clue. Our prior knowledge tells us that when there are dark clouds, there is often rain. Then, we might infer: *I think I should take an umbrella today.* Smelling sweet chocolate smells coming from the kitchen is a clue. Our prior knowledge tells us that sweet chocolate smells often mean someone is baking cookies. Then, we can infer: *I think chocolate cookies may be ready soon.*

Information in the book or picture (clues) + **Prior Knowledge** = **Inference**

A powerful way to begin inferring with fiction is through wordless books, photographs, or illustrations. With these visual texts, combining clues in the picture(s) and our background knowledge helps us make sense of stories.

For example, in a version of *The Three Little Pigs*, the illustration shows the first little pig building his house of straw while the wolf hides in the bushes, licking his lips. The text never mentions the wolf. In working with striving readers, we might say: *Look at the wolf. He is watching the little pig and licking his lips. It doesn't say so in the book, but I can infer that he is thinking about eating the pig! When I look at the house, I can make another inference. I know straw is dried grass. It doesn't say this in the book, but I know that grass can blow away in the wind. It can be easily pushed around and moved. It can even catch on fire and burn. I can infer that this house won't last very long. Straw isn't a good material to use in building a house. Readers, do you notice how I use clues in the pictures and my knowledge about the world to infer? I use the stem* I can infer *because that identifies the important thinking that I am doing in my head.*

Readers work together to infer and reach deeper understanding.

Some great examples to consider for inferring from illustrations are wordless books such as the *Good Dog, Carl* series by Alexandra Day, *The Snowman* by Raymond Briggs, *Pancakes for Breakfast* by Tomie dePaola, *Flotsam* (a Caldecott medal winner) by David Wiesner, or the partially wordless, *Rosie's Walk* by Pat Hutchins.

Beginning inferences are often about the characters or events in the story, but additionally we want to take readers to a higher level and make inferences about the big messages in a story—the themes and lessons learned along the way. Inferring can help readers dig deeper into their thoughts and discover ideas that go beyond the literal level—to lessons about life.

Steps for *I Can Infer*

1. Begin with *Rosie's Walk* or another book of your selection and a poster showing the equation "clues + prior knowledge = inference." Think aloud about gathering clues and adding prior knowledge. An example: *On the first page, I can see Rosie the hen taking a walk and the fox watching her from under the henhouse. His tongue is hanging out. That is a clue. I know that foxes like to eat chickens so I can infer that he is going to try to catch her. On the next page, I see the fox is leaping in the air and there is a rake on the ground. These are clues. My prior knowledge tells me that if you step on the tines of a rake, the handle will pop up and smack you in the head. I can infer that the fox is going to be hit by the handle of the rake. Let's turn the page and see.*

2. On the next page, have students look closely at the position of the fox and the pond. Help them identify clues about what might happen to the fox and use prior knowledge. Then, using the stem I Can Infer, have partners generate statements about what is likely to happen next.

3. Continue guided practice in generating inferences with several different selections until your striving readers build confidence with inference.

4. Have partners work together on a familiar text to share their inferences, and record them on sticky notes for a later group share.

5. As individuals read independently, have them record inferences on sticky notes to share with thinking partners.

SOLUTION to Question #2 FICTION

Whole Class OR **Small Group**

Partners

Two-Word Strategy

The Two-Word Strategy (Hoyt 2009b) is a powerful *solution* for helping striving readers experience "beyond the text" thinking and inferential reasoning. To infer, readers must take clues in the text, merge them with prior knowledge, and then generate thinking that is uniquely their own. It is helpful to shape directions to the students carefully and ask them to generate two words that reflect their thinking about the text. If you ask readers to identify two words *from* the text, this experience will drop down to literal-level thinking. The Two-Word Strategy is not meant to be a time-filler but rather a springboard to reflective writing and conversation, so be sure to follow the generation of words with lots of conversation and writing. Some examples:

The wolf in the *Three Little Pigs*: *The wolf was very* hungry *or he would have given up on the pigs. It was amazing that he was so* determined *to catch them.*

hungry	**determined**

The entire book, *Stone Fox*: *The book Stone Fox by Gardiner is filled with moments where both Searchlight and Little Willy proved they were* courageous *as they worked together to save the farm. While the loss of Searchlight was* heartbreaking, *it was clear that Little Willy had the strength to move forward with his life.*

courageous	**heartbreaking**

The book *Click, Clack, Moo and Cows That Type*: Click, Clack, Moo *was really* funny. *While I know that it is not real and that cows and ducks can't type, it was great to think about the problem from their* point of view.

funny	**point of view**

Steps for *Two-Word Strategy*

1. Gather a full class or small group and post a chart with two boxes spaced across the top of the page. After reading a book that your students were able to comprehend comfortably, model how you think about the book and generate two words that *reflect your thinking about the text*. Write one word in each box on the chart, then tell students why you chose them. Explain that *none* of the words are in the book, they are inferences you created by thinking about the book.

2. Model and think aloud as you draft a sentence or two about the book, making sure that you use the two target words in your writing. For each target word, be sure that it is underlined or presented as boldfaced type so it stands out within the sentence.

3. Provide an opportunity for partners to generate two words about the book.

4. Present a familiar book to a small group of striving readers, then mentor and coach as they apply the Two-Word Strategy with partners, using a text at their independent reading level.

5. Provide an opportunity for partners to talk about the words they selected and how they relate to the story.

6. Finally, engage your students in writing about the story and including the two words they identified.

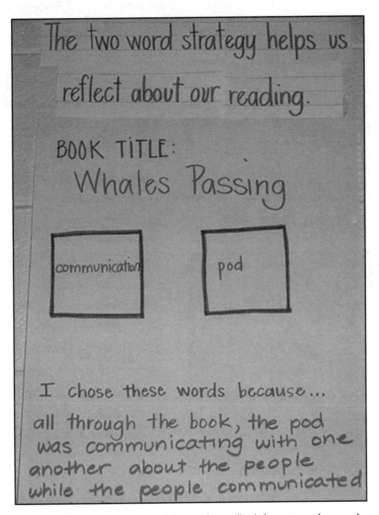

The Two-Word Strategy helps striving readers utilize inferences as they reach for deeper understanding.

Inference Equation

Inference equations are a *solution* designed to help striving readers notice and clarify relationships between ideas and concepts. Using the format of a mathematical equation, relationships between characters and situations are highlighted and inferences are generated. A key feature of inference equations is to have striving readers explain the thinking that supports the equation by pointing out why their equation is important to understanding the story. Some examples:

Goldilocks + A Nap = Discovery by the Bears
(*This is important because the bears needed to know who broke into their house.*)

Cinderella + a Mean Stepmother = A Stressed Out Cleaning Lady
(*This is important because Cinderella's stepmother was very cruel and gave the stepsisters nice things while Cinderella worked and cleaned and had to wear rags.*)

Little Willy − Searchlight = A Brokenhearted Boy
(*This is important because Little Willy loved Searchlight so much. When Searchlight died, Willy must have been so sad.*)

Little Willy × Determination = Harvested Potatoes and a Winning Race
(*This is important because Little Willy worked hard and did things most kids normally can't do. He saved the farm because he had so much determination.*)

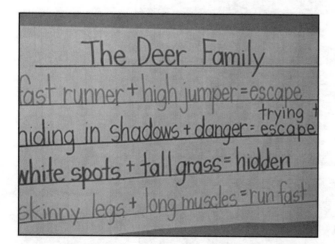

Inference equations help striving readers to see relationships between isolated facts and concepts.

Steps for *Inference Equation*

1. Create several opportunities to model the creation of inference equations (after small-group interactions with a leveled selection, a whole-class read-aloud, or a shared reading experience). Think aloud as you construct an equation so striving readers can hear you think about a character and his attributes or consider an event from the story. Point out that the equation is not in the book, so readers need to do their own thinking to create an inference equation. Over several sessions, model equations using different mathematical functions.

2. Once your striving readers catch onto the format, have partners create inference equations on sentence strips to share with others.

3. As confidence grows, have students create inference equations about books they are reading independently and share them with partners.

Whole Class OR **Small Group**

Partners

Independent

Question-Generating Strategy

Striving readers benefit from opportunities to generate questions before reading, during reading, and after reading. These questions might be based on pictures in the text, knowledge of the genre, familiarity with the author, puzzling events, or character motivation. What is important in this *solution* is that there is a constant flow of questions throughout the reading event. This flow of questions increases reader engagement and stimulates intrinsic motivation. If a book is a mystery and readers have some experience reading mysteries, they might generate questions such as: *What clues will I discover as I read? What will the mystery be? How will the characters solve the mystery?* If the text is a biography, typical questions might be: *What did this person do to earn recognition? What was this person like as a child? What events in their childhood led them to become a special adult?* If the book is realistic fiction questions might be: *Where does this story take place? How will the main character change throughout the book? Are there similarities between this character's life and mine?*

As readers delve into texts, they should be encouraged to stop at various points and record or reflect on their questions. They may find answers to their questions as they read. They may discover that answers remain unclear and invite shared wondering between partners or in a small group. The important thing is for readers to be actively engaged in thinking and questioning before, during, and after reading.

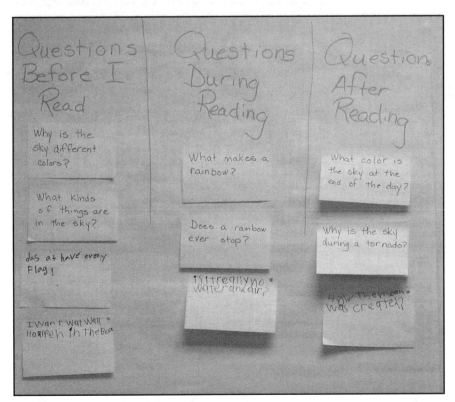

Evidence suggests that when striving readers generate questions before, during, and after reading, they remember more and experience deeper levels of engagement.

As with all supportive instruction, modeling is essential and serves as a springboard as striving readers reach for higher levels of proficiency.

Steps for *Question-Generating Strategy*

1. Create and post a three-column chart labeled Questions Before, Questions During, and Questions After Reading.

2. Select an interesting short text or passage to read aloud for a whole class or a small group, modeling how to pause frequently and generate questions before reading. Questions can be based on the title, knowledge about the author, genre, cover, or illustrations. Begin with just two or three questions, writing questions on sticky notes, and posting them in the Before Reading column.

3. As you read the passage, pause two or three times to generate further questions or to point out that a before reading question has been answered. Record during-reading questions on sticky notes and put them on the column of the chart labeled Questions During.

4. After reading, stop and generate postreading questions based on the passage. *I wonder if the author thought about _____? The author forgot to tell what happened to _____. I wonder what happened.* Record those questions on sticky notes and add to the chart in the After Reading column.

5. Provide an opportunity for partners to generate before-, during-, and after-reading questions related to a book at their independent reading level.

6. As your striving students demonstrate understanding of the interactive questioning process, provide guided practice with a shared text (big book or enlargement on a document camera). In this supportive context, you can read sections of the passage and have partners generate questions of their own.

7. Finally, have students utilize personal questioning charts focused on guided or independent reading selections and then share their questions with a partner.

Small Group

Partners

Independent

Quality Questions: Coaching for Layers of Understanding

Striving readers need to become questioning experts, learning to flexibly handle questions of many types whether the questions are generated by a text, a teacher, a testing situation, their peers, or themselves. In this *solution*, the goal is to coach striving students to become highly knowledgeable about questions, identifying those that are literal, those that are open-ended and invite thinking, and those that are critical or analytical in nature. It falls upon us, as their coaches and mentors, to ask questions that help striving readers explore layers of meaning, while also encouraging them to delve deeply into their own sense of wonder as they generate questions of their own.

Although there will always be a place for literal, right-or-wrong questions, we must remember that such questions will not lead to insightful thinking and won't support lively discussion. As coaches, we also need to give readers opportunities to both respond to and create questions that don't have a single right answer. Thoughtfully constructed questions clarify confusing ideas, challenge thinking, or open the possibility of another viewpoint. Thoughtfully constructed questions, either those of a teacher or those that striving readers construct, need to reflect layers of understanding and help striving readers to see the world with fresh eyes.

Striving readers need to generate and experience questions representing many layers of understanding.

P. David Pearson (2008) suggests that questions may be organized into three supportive categories: aesthetic, efferent, and critical/analytical. Aesthetic questions are those that help readers respond to a story and share their thinking. These questions invite opinions, connections, or personal response. This is good news for striving readers as evidence suggests they may benefit from opportunities to respond to reading selections emotionally before moving to the facts (Allington 2010). Efferent questions are those that focus on unpacking the facts—retelling and summarizing—without adding personal bias or opinion. They help us compare and contrast and think about story structure, story elements, point of view, and important ideas. Critical/analytical questions engage striving students in interrogating the text, questioning the author, and analyzing elements of craft or the purpose of the author. Critical/analytical

Quality Questions also appears on the CD.

responses may also involve evaluation and judgment. By addressing all three levels of questions, we coach and mentor students via powerful conversations that stimulate deep thinking. As you review the provided list of questions, keep in mind that you will want to adjust and modify the questions according to the age, level of literacy development, and English language proficiency of your students. The primary goal is not for learners to label the question types, but rather to have the advantage they will gain when you, as their mentor, ensure that each striving reader gets to experience multifaceted layers of meaning.

Steps for *Quality Questions: Coaching for Layers of Understanding*

1. In a small-group setting, explain to your striving readers that when you create questions for them, you are careful to include questions that focus on different types of thinking. Using a familiar read-aloud, create a chart on which you model writing questions that focus on Responding (aesthetic), Reporting (efferent), and Evaluating (critical/analytical). Think aloud about what a reader needs to do to answer each one, and explain that questions of different types help readers to think about text in a variety of ways.

2. Invite students to converse in partner pairs and add questions to each category. The process of generating questions will expand language proficiency and deepen comprehension.

3. Have partners work together to create questions that are aesthetic, efferent, and analytical, after reading a leveled section at their independent level. Then, form groups of four and have the students share their questions with each other, reflecting on which questions best helped them understand the story.

4. As students continue to mature in their understanding of questions, provide opportunities for them to develop questions about independent reading selections. They may want to post their questions inside of books used for independent reading so the next reader can also engage with your students' questions.

Quality Questions

Responding (Aesthetic) Expressive Responses That Invite Learners to Share Their Thinking

How did you feel?

What did you wonder?

What was your favorite part? Why?

Which character did you find most intriguing? Why?

If you were the author, which part of the story would bring you the most pride?

Are there any parts of this selection that you would change?

At which points were you best able to visualize or "see" the action?

What did the author do that helped you connect to this selection?

What did you learn?

Reporting (Efferent): Unpacking the Facts of the Text

Who, what, when, where?

In what order?

Which characters are central to the story?

Describe the climax.

From which point of view is this selection written?

If we were to identify the most important ideas, what would they be?

Compare the events in this story with the events in _____.

Evaluating (Critical/Analytical): Students Interrogate the Text, the Author, the Issue, and the Purpose

What important issues were addressed in this selection? Why are these important?

What does the author want you to believe or understand? What is the author's point of view?

What do you think was the author's message or theme?

If we were to evaluate this selection, what criteria might we consider?

Adapted from Linda Hoyt, Revisit, Reflect, Retell, Updated Edition, © 2009. Portsmouth, NH: Heinemann. Used with permission. May be photocopied for classroom use only.

 OR

Whole Class   Small Group

Partners

Independent

I Wonder also appears on the CD.

I Wonder

This *solution* provides an easy entry for striving readers as they learn to engage more deeply with personal questions. The idea is to focus on I Wonder questions before, during, and after reading to activate a dialogue between readers and the selections they are reading. This facilitates language use, activates prior knowledge, and elevates engagement.

Steps for *I Wonder*

1. During a whole-class or small-group read-aloud, model how you approach a text with a sense of wonder. Let your readers listen as you ask questions about the cover, the title, the interior visuals, and the first pages of the selection.

2. Make it clear that you don't expect immediate answers to your questions. Your questions are, instead, helping you connect with the text and think more deeply about layers of meaning.

3. Create distinct pauses for I Wonder questions before, during, and after reading the selection.

4. Have striving readers work in partner pairs or independently to engage with I Wonder in a wide variety of reading selections at their independent reading level. With each selection, coach them in pausing to generate I Wonder questions.

Striving readers thrive when they have opportunities to generate their own questions and interact with the text.

I Wonder

Reader 1 _____   Reader 2 _____

Focus Book _____

Preview a fiction selection. Read the title and examine the pictures. Read just the *first* page.

1. Think of an I Wonder question. Write it down.

   I wonder _____

   _____

   _____

   _____

   ➡️ **I found the answer!**
   When you find an answer to a question, write it here.

2. Read one or two more pages, ask yourself another I Wonder question, then read to find the answer.

   I wonder _____

   _____

   _____

   _____

   ➡️ **I found the answer!**
   When you find an answer to a question, write it here.

3. Additional Questions

   I wonder _____

   _____

   _____

   _____

   ➡️ **I found the answer!**
   When you find an answer to a question, write it here.

4. Write or draw to show the most important ideas you discovered.

Whole Class   OR   Small Group

Partners

Connecting to Fiction Selections

Connections help striving readers identify with the characters and situations in a story. When striving readers empathize with characters, recognize situations they have encountered, or draw generalizations regarding common features of people and cultures, they activate prior knowledge and comprehension improves (Au 2010; Krashen 2003; Boushey and Moser 2006; Chard, Vaughn, and Tyler 2002).

Three levels of connection are commonly recommended: text to self, text to world, text to text. In text-to-self connections, personal memories and experiences are linked to the text. In text-to-world connections, content knowledge about butterflies, snakes, weather patterns, and so on inform and support reader understanding. In text-to-text connections, readers compare and contrast the text they are currently reading with one they have read in the past.

A caution: We have found that in making connections, young readers often find connections with little relevance to the storyline, like "My grandma's next-door neighbor likes to go fishing." At that point, we gently remind readers that our connections should help us understand the story better and we always ask ourselves, "How does my connection help me understand the story?"

Students discuss personal connections to the book they are reading.

Steps for *Connecting to Fiction Selections*

1. Choose a read-aloud book that has connections that fit both you and your students.

2. As you read to a whole class or small group, think aloud about how you connect to the people or situations in the story. Be sure to tell the students how your connections help you to understand the story better. You may want to model having an irrelevant or distracting connection to show young readers how you discard such thoughts and return to the core of the text (Zemelman, Daniels, and Hyde 2012).

3. As you progress through the text, have readers practice making connections with a partner, recording their helpful connections on sticky notes.

4. Organize partners into groups of four to have a conversation about connections they discovered and how their connections helped them to understand the story better.

 OR

Whole Class   **Small Group**

Partners

Independent

QAR (Question–Answer Relationships)

QAR is a framework that supports striving readers in understanding that answers to questions can be derived in several ways (Raphael and Au 2005; Raphael, Highfield, and Au 2006). The goal is to help striving readers to understand that questions can be answered:

In the book: The answer is at a specific point in the text or in a collection of information throughout the text.

In my head: A reader uses background knowledge in concert with text clues to create an inference or answers questions using prior knowledge alone.

By creating common language and making these text demands visible to readers, the authors of QAR have created a system that supports readers as they seek to answer questions.

For older students who become proficient with in-the-book and in-my-head questions, additional categories can become useful. *Right there* implies that the answer can be found in one place in the text. *Think and search* implies that the reader must collect bits of information throughout the text and synthesize the answer. *Author and me* indicates that the text has part of the information but the reader must also use background knowledge and

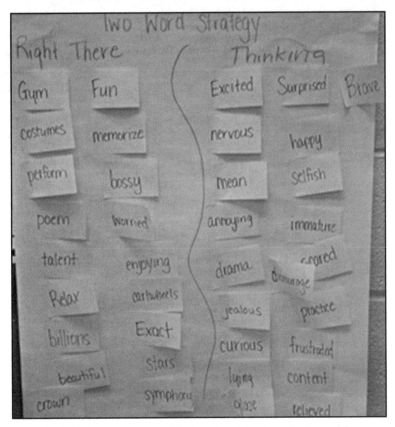

It may be helpful to start with individual words related to a selection and then move to ideas. As you can see in this picture, the teacher had striving readers generate words, which they then sorted to identify their source.

infer to answer. *On my own* cues striving readers that the answer does not come from the text but completely from their own thinking such as in opinions and judgments. As you engage with this *solution*, help striving readers understand that identifying these questioning categories can help them navigate assignments and even standardized tests more effectively.

An example from *Goldilocks and the Three Bears*

In the Book	In My Head
Right there: What did Goldilocks eat at the bears' house?	Author and me: How do you think Baby Bear felt when he discovered his broken chair?
Think and search: Tell two or three things Goldilocks did that were naughty.	On my own: Why shouldn't you go into someone's house without permission?

Steps for *QAR*

1. Gather the whole class or a small group. Create a T-chart labeled In the Book and In My Head. Read a familiar story to the students and model how to create questions for which answers are *in* the book and questions that need to come from *thinking about* the book. Record questions in the appropriate columns.

An example: Goldilocks. Where did Goldilocks take her nap?

In the Book	In My Head
On Baby Bear's bed.	That was rude. Perhaps her mother forgot to teach her to wait until she is invited.

2. Engage students in a discussion about the questions and the strategies you used to locate answers. Have partners contribute additional questions that fit each category.

3. After students read short passages that you are sure they understand, ask partners to respond to a small number of prepared questions by deciding which questions can be answered directly in the book and which ones require them to think about the book. In-the-book answers can be marked with sticky notes.

4. Over time, have students read additional passages and practice generating their own in-the-book or in-my-head questions about their reading. It is important for students to learn how to respond to prepared questions as well as generate questions of their own.

What Oral and Written Responses Help Striving Learners Deepen Understanding of Fiction?

Side-by-Side Observation: Angelina

Angelina, a second grader, is learning English as an additional language. Language for interpersonal communication is firmly in place, and current efforts have focused on expanding her cognitive academic language and improving her ability to engage in oral and written responses to literature. Story maps, oral retells, and written responses indicate that Angelina has a basic understanding of story structure but needs additional scaffolds to deepen her reflections on fiction, especially as related to character development. It is clear that she is most comfortable when she has an opportunity to draw or use drama before she engages in small-group conversations or written response. After analyzing anecdotal notes, comprehension checklists, and writing samples and doing an observation of oral language, we decide to provide Angelina with more opportunities to mediate her learning through dramatic reenactment in whole-class and small-group settings and be especially sure that fiction selections are set in sociocultural environments that are familiar to her. In addition, we will ensure that Angelina is engaged with open-ended questions to stimulate language use and provided with language stems to assist her in partner conversations. Written response and opportunities to deepen character analysis offer additional learning targets for this striving reader.

Formative Assessment Tools

⇨ Story Mapping Graphic Organizers, pages 91–92

⇨ Observation of Oral Language, page 171

⇨ Fiction Retell Checklist, page 182

⇨ Individual Conference Notes, page 151

Data collection must include a range of formative assessments to ensure a broad-based understanding of learner development.

We Notice . . . In reflecting on formative assessments, observations, and an interview with Angelina, we notice:

- Story maps, the comprehension checklist, and written responses show that Angelina understands fiction story structure but needs guidance in deeper thinking.

- Angelina has difficulty sustaining conversations focused on deep thinking and needs access to and support with language stems for deeper conversations.
- She needs experiences in identifying character traits and expressing understanding of the story in writing.

We Will Try . . . To help striving readers like Angelina think more deeply about fiction and move forward as a language user, we offer the following suggestions.

Conversation Stems page 124	Picture This page 126	ACT It Out! page 128	Character Traits page 129

Whole Class   Small Group   Partners

Whole Class   Small Group   Partners   Independent

Whole Class   Small Group   Partners

Whole Class   Small Group   Partners

Additional Solutions to Consider

Character Comparisons page 134	If I Were the Author page 136	Memorable Moments page 138

Whole Class   Small Group   Partners

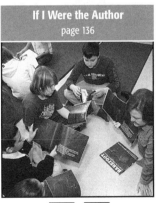

Small Group   Partners

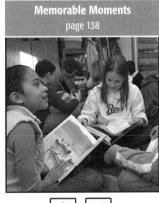

Small Group   Partners

Whole Class OR **Small Group**

Partners

Conversation Stems appears full size on the CD.

Conversation Stems for Fiction

Striving readers, including English language learners, may have difficulty sustaining a partner or small-group discussion because they do not have a richly developed arsenal of the conversation stems that extend and support conversations. In this *solution*, we mentor striving readers in broadening the range of conversation stems they utilize by collaboratively developing charts of language stems. We recommend that you coconstruct an anchor chart with a limited number of stems. As striving readers gain linguistic confidence with the initial stems, add new stems so conversations are reenergized and expanded each time the anchor chart is revisited. Be sure the chart is visually accessible so your striving readers can refer to it as they engage in partner conversations or small-group discussions across the curriculum. Here we offer some suggestions from which to select stems that best match your striving readers.

Striving readers accelerate independence, social interaction, thinking, and language proficiency when conversation stems support partner work.

Conversation Stems to Sustain and Extend Conversations: Partners and Small Groups

Your comment makes me wonder . . .	I'd love to hear more about your thinking on that . . .	The character changed when . . .	I'm glad the author . . .
Your comment reminds me that . . .	I wonder . . .	I predict . . .	What makes this character real is . . .
What did you think about . . .	I think . . .	I think it means . . .	This part is not realistic because . . .
What led you to that line of thinking?	I liked . . .	Why did . . .	I felt like I was part of the story when . . .
What did you notice in the text that supports your idea?	My favorite part was . . .	What would happen if . . .	I'm picturing . . .
I can "link up" to that thought.	I didn't like . . .	Do you think . . .	This is like . . .
	I realized . . .	What part did you like best? Why?	The setting reminds me of . . .
	The story reminded me of . . .	This is confusing because . . .	The lesson or theme that stands out to me is . . .
	If I were the author, I would have . . .	This part seems very real because . . .	

Steps for *Conversation Stems for Fiction*

1. Post a chart with a limited number of stems and ask a student to be your partner for a demonstration for the whole class or a small group. Focusing on a book that is familiar, consciously attempt to utilize stems on the chart to energize and empower your thinking. Pause occasionally to walk to the chart, read, and then return to your partner. Let your striving readers see how you actively use the chart to scaffold your conversation. Invite group members to suggest stems that you and your partner might use to keep the conversation going.

2. Engage the observing students in partner discussion about how the chart of stems helped the conversation go deeper and coach them in selecting a few additional stems to add.

3. Provide opportunities for striving readers to engage in partner conversations and small-group conversations in which they consciously use the stems to extend and enrich their literate conversation. (Some striving readers may find it helpful to prepare sticky notes with stems they especially want to use and place them on a clipboard or on the table in front of them.)

4. Treat the chart of stems as a fluid, interactive scaffold by continually adding stems, deleting those that students do not find to be helpful, and so on.

Conversation stems can help striving readers have literate conversations that are thought provoking and satisfying.

 OR

Whole Class   **Small Group**

Partners

Independent

Picture This

Sensory imaging elevates engagement and serves as a powerful support to comprehension. In addition, studies have shown that sensory imaging supports language acquisition as it gives striving readers an opportunity to personalize content, making it concrete and comprehensible (Cloud, Genese, and Hamayan 2009; Pressley 2002; Siegel 1985).

So, it is essential that striving readers have intentionally crafted opportunities to visualize—to consider smells and textures, or the sounds that they would hear if they were to enter a setting highlighted in a book. In this age of computers, videos, television, and video games, students have less reason to engage in sensory imaging, especially visualization, because technology inundates them with so many visual images (Willis 2007; Keene and Zimmerman 2007). Therefore, we need to provide striving readers with explicit opportunities to create their own sensory images as they listen to and read narrative text. We can support them by asking: *What do you see, smell, taste, feel, and hear?* We can ask them to describe scenes and actions in read-alouds, or close their eyes and consciously focus on creating images in their minds.

When striving readers pause and consciously visualize settings and situations described in a book, they remember more and are better prepared to engage in thoughtful dialogue.

If we, as mentors and coaches to striving readers, take the importance of visualization very seriously and teach it with great intentionality, evidence suggests that comprehension will improve. The mental imagery that we experience while reading, either spontaneously or induced by instruction, is now known to have powerful effects on comprehension, memory, and appreciation for text. In this *solution*, striving readers learn how to consciously activate sensory imaging and use it to solidify understanding.

Steps for *Picture This*

1. Select picture books with rich sensory images such as *Owl Moon* by Jane Yolen, *Stellaluna* by Janelle Cannon, *Bat Loves the Night* by Nicole Davies, or *Dogteam* by Gary Paulson.

2. Read one selection to your students (the whole class or small group), but do not show them the illustrations. Pause often to have readers close their eyes and visualize as you read. After each pause, provide partners with an opportunity to talk about the details that they visualized and focus on elements of the setting that became clear to them as they paused to *see* within their mind's eye.

As striving readers become proficient in sensory imaging, they experience a stream of images—like a movie in their head.

3. After reading, have learners sketch the setting and write about the rich images they drew from the reading selection. Then, share with a partner.

4. Show striving readers the original illustrations in the published book and discuss how their own visualizations were alike, different, or even better than the ones in the book!

5. As learners gain proficiency, have them read passages independently and sketch what they envision before writing and describing the scene.

6. Share visualizations and writing with partners or small groups. Talk about what people and places and experiences served as a basis for our sensory image.

ACT It Out! is fun and engaging for striving readers of all ages. Vocabulary, oral language, and comprehension come together in the most positive of ways.

ACT It Out!

Dramatic enactments enliven and engage striving readers in ways that sitting at a desk could never accomplish. Because enactments and action strategies involve movement, the natural desire to move creates links to memory and thoughtful reflection (Jenson 2005; Willis 2007; Gill 2008; Steineke 2010). Best of all, action strategies and enactments have been thoroughly proven to improve both motivation and comprehension for vulnerable and reluctant learners (Smith and Wilhelm 2002; Valde and Kornetsky 2002).

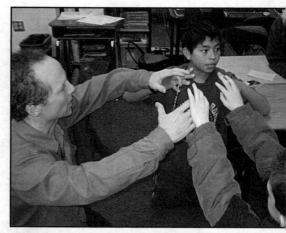

When striving readers pause and consciously visualize settings and situations described in a book, they remember more and are better prepared to engage in thoughtful dialogue.

In the *solution* ACT It Out! striving readers create a list of character descriptors. Then, they work with partners to dramatize the descriptors as applied to the focus character. They might dramatize just the descriptive word, or they might elect to dramatize a scene in which the character behaved in this way. In Goldilocks and the Three Bears, Goldilocks could be described as *rude, untrustworthy, willful, bold, sleepy, hungry,* or *mischievous.* These words are posted, then partner pairs plan, practice, and present their dramatizations while the other team members try to guess which descriptor is being enacted. With ACT It Out! experiences, striving readers reach for deeper understanding, expand oral language proficiency, and enliven vocabulary.

Steps for *ACT It Out!*

1. Post a list of descriptors for a familiar fiction character, and then demonstrate how to dramatize one of the words as the whole class or a small group observes. Students consider the posted list, observe your enactment, then select the character description that matches.

2. Invite partners to examine the list and select a different descriptor to enact. After they have a chance to practice, provide an opportunity to present for others.

3. As striving readers develop expertise with ACT It Out! provide opportunities for them to return to a text and present evidence in the text supporting their dramatization.

4. Consider extending ACT It Out! by having striving learners write about the descriptions and scenes they enacted.

OR

Whole Class   Small Group

Partners

Understanding Character Traits

Striving learners need to be taught that proficient readers must pay close attention to the behaviors of a character—not just the events—in a story. The goal of this *solution* is to coach striving readers in how to notice a character's responses to different situations, then to look for insights about the character's inner personality. It may be helpful to begin this conversation by describing a real student in the class or group, then transfer your think-aloud to a story that is familiar to the students.

Your think-aloud might sound something like:

I noticed that Elina took time to pick up all the coats that fell on the floor after lunch and hang them back on their hooks. Based on her actions, I can say that Elina has the trait of being very helpful.

Andreas, I have noticed that every day you take a moment to rearrange your desk so that everything is neat. Based on your concern about your desk, I could say that you have the traits of being organized and tidy.

Michael, when I look at you, no matter what has happened, you are smiling. You make the best of situations that would make a lot of us feel sad. Based on the way you act, I could say that you are a very positive person.

Let's think about the behaviors of Brian in Hatchet. We know that Brian invented a lot of tools to help himself survive. He carved a spear and attached a sharp point to the end. He devised a way to collect and drink water. And, he figured out how to stay warm even though he didn't have a blanket. Based on Brian's actions in Hatchet, I could say that he had the trait of being very creative.

As you work with character traits, you will discover that you are expanding vocabulary and coaching striving readers to use character behaviors to identify their traits.

Steps for *Understanding Character Traits*

1. Post a small number of character traits on an anchor chart. During a whole-class read-aloud or a small-group reading experience, pause often to identify behaviors of the character and model how to select descriptive traits from the chart. Ideally, there will be times when you don't find the perfect trait listed, so you can add to the list of character attributes as the story unfolds.

2. Have partners think together and identify the character traits they think *best* describe a character and justify their thinking with examples from the story.

Understanding Character Traits and *Character Traits Organizer* also appear on the CD.

3. Learners may want to use writer's notebooks to create their own Character Trait charts using the descriptors they have identified and evidence from the text—adding to their lists of traits over time, just as you have modeled with the anchor chart.

4. Offer partners plentiful opportunities to talk together about character behaviors and descriptive traits.

Striving readers learn to identify character traits when they are coached to notice the behaviors of characters rather than simply tracking story events.

Sample List of Character Traits also appears on the CD.

We offer a fairly comprehensive list of character traits here as a teacher reference. This is not intended for student use.

Understanding Character Traits

Reader _____ Book _____ Date _____

Character _____

I think this character is _____ and _____ because _____

_____

_____

Character _____

I think this character is _____ and _____ because _____

_____

_____

Character _____

I think this character is _____ and _____ because _____

_____

_____

Character Traits Organizer

Character Name_____

Trait   **Revealed by . . .**

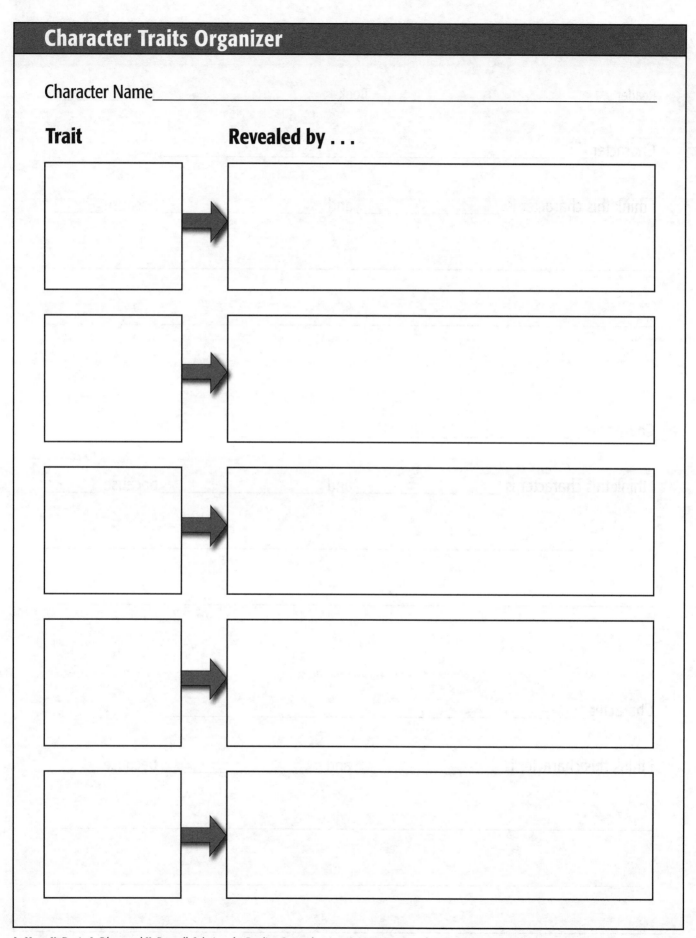

L. Hoyt, K. Davis, J. Olson, and K. Boswell, Solutions for Reading Comprehension, © 2011. Portsmouth, NH: Heinemann. May be photocopied for classroom use only.

Sample List of Character Traits

able, absent-minded, active, adaptable, adventurous, affable, affectionate, afraid, alert, ambitious, amiable, angry, animated, annoyed, anxious, apologetic, argumentative, arrogant, attentive, average, awkward, babyish, bad, blue, boastful, bold, bored, bossy, brainy, brave, bright, brilliant, busy, calm, candid, capable, careful, careless, carefree, caring, caustic, cautious, changeable, charismatic, charming, cheerful, childish, clever, clumsy, coarse, coldhearted, compassionate, complacent, conceited, concerned, confident, confused, contented, conscientious, considerate, cooperative, courageous, cowardly, crafty, critical, cross, creative, cruel, cultured, curious, dainty, dangerous, daring, dark, dauntless, decisive, demanding, dependable, depressed, determined, diligent, disagreeable, discouraged, discreet, dishonest, disrespectful, domineering, doubtful, dreamer, dull, dutiful, eager, easygoing, effervescent, efficient, eloquent, embarrassed, encouraging, energetic, enthusiastic, evil, exacting, excited, expert, exuberant, facetious, fair, faithful, fancy, fearful, fearless, fierce, fighter, finicky, foolish, forgetful, forgiving, formal, fortunate, foul, frank, fresh, friendly, frustrated, fun-loving, funny, fussy, garrulous, generous, gentle, giddy, giving, glamorous, gloomy, glum, good, graceful, grateful, greedy, gregarious, grouchy, grumpy, guilty, gullible, handsome, happy, hardy, hardworking, harried, harsh, hateful, haughty, healthy, helpful, honest, hopeful, hopeless, hospitable, humble, humorous, ignorant, imaginative, immaculate, immature, impartial, impatient, impolite, impudent, impulsive, inconsiderate, independent, industrious, innocent, insolent, intelligent, intrepid, inventive, jealous, jolly, jovial, joyful, kind, kindly, keen, lackadaisical, languid, lazy, leader, lighthearted, lively, logical, lonely, loquacious, loud, lovable, loving, loyal, lucky, malicious, mannerly, mature, mean, messy, mischievous, miserable, moody, mysterious, nagging, naïve, naughty, neat, negligent, nervous, nice, noisy, nurturing, obedient, obliging, obnoxious, old, organized, outspoken, patient, patriotic, peaceful, picky, pitiful, plain, playful, pleasant, polite, poor, popular, positive, precise, prim, proper, proud, quarrelsome, quick, quick-tempered, quiet, rational, reasonable, reckless, relaxed, reliable, religious, reserved, resourceful, respectful, responsible, restless, rich, rough, rowdy, rude, sad, safe, satisfied, scared, secretive, self-centered, self-confident, selfish, sensitive, sentimental, serious, sharp, sharp-witted, shiftless, short, shrewd, shy, silly, simple, skillful, sly, smart, sneaky, softhearted, spunky, sorry, spoiled, stern, stingy, studious, strange, strict, strong, stubborn, successful, superstitious, suspicious, sweet, talented, talkative, tall, thankful, thoughtful, thoughtless, timid, tired, tireless, tolerant, touchy, tough, trusting, trustworthy, understanding, unfriendly, unhappy, unkind, unselfish, upset, useful, warm, weak, wicked, wild, wise, witty, worried, wrong, young, zany

L. Hoyt, K. Davis, J. Olson, and K. Boswell, Solutions for Reading Comprehension, © 2011. Portsmouth, NH: Heinemann. *May be photocopied for classroom use only.*

 OR

Whole Class   **Small Group**

Partners

Character Comparisons

Venn diagrams certainly fall into the category of "tried and true," but they are worth dusting off and bringing forward for your striving readers. With Venn diagrams, vulnerable readers have strong visual support as they compare characters and their attributes. In this *solution*, striving readers may want to compare two characters within a selection, characters from different books, or a character in a story to themselves. Compare-and-contrast experiences have been found to be strongly correlated to increased comprehension and language competence as the visual nature of Venn diagrams provides substantial support to striving readers (Dragan 2005; Dreher and Gray 2009; Klingner, Vaughn, and Boardman 2007).

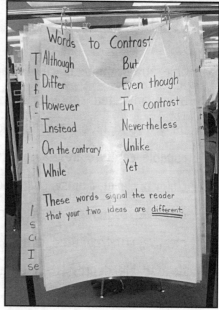

Connecting words add sophistication to the writing of striving readers.

Steps for *Character Comparisons*

1. Choose two familiar characters that have similarities and differences.

2. Create a Venn diagram by drawing two intersecting circles on a chart. The overlap of the circles is where you record attributes that the two characters have in common. The separate circles are where you record things that apply to one character, but not the other.

3. As your whole class or a small group observes, model how to identify traits and attributes, then place them in the appropriate sections of the diagram, making sure you show your striving readers how to return to the book to check illustrations and text for additional details and/or justification for the attributes you are listing.

4. Model how to create a descriptive piece of writing based on the attributes listed on the chart, adding justifications from the text.

5. Invite striving readers to create Venn diagrams with partners, adding character traits and attributes related to different characters. Be sure they have an opportunity to use their attributes in a piece of descriptive writing.

6. As your striving readers appear ready to add sophistication to their writing, try showing them how to use connecting words and phrases that reflect comparison such as: *but, although, on the other hand, similarly, also, different from, similar to, even though,* and so on.

Hula hoops provide a tactile frame and moveable sticky notes invite kinesthetic action.

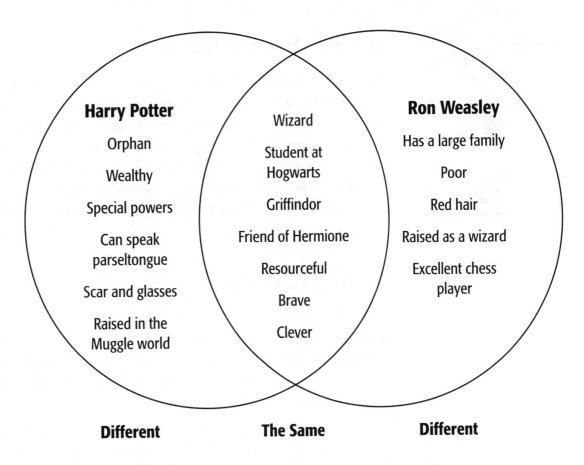

Harry Potter

Orphan

Wealthy

Special powers

Can speak parseltongue

Scar and glasses

Raised in the Muggle world

Wizard

Student at Hogwarts

Griffindor

Friend of Hermione

Resourceful

Brave

Clever

Ron Weasley

Has a large family

Poor

Red hair

Raised as a wizard

Excellent chess player

Different   **The Same**   **Different**

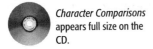

Character Comparisons appears full size on the CD.

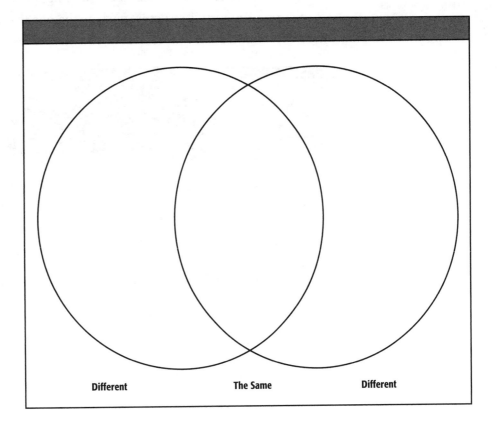

Different   The Same   Different

Small Group

Partners

If I Were the Author

If I Were the Author provides striving readers with opportunities to take a critical/analytical stance and offer opinions and personal reflections on stories they have read. This is empowering as there are no wrong answers and kids love opportunities to critique. The objective of this *solution* is to think like an evaluator and wonder: *If I had been the author, what would I be proud of? What might I want to change about the story, the way a character is described, or the setting? How would I rate the author's action verbs and precise nouns? If I were the author, would I have made the characters any different?* and so on.

Steps for *If I Were the Author*

1. Gather a small group for a guided reading experience.

2. After reading, use the stem If I Were the Author and model how to think aloud about the selection. You might offer compliments to the author, make suggestions about the storyline, or point out something unique about the lead or the ending.

3. Give partners an opportunity to use the stem If I Were the Author and prepare comments to orally share with another partner pair.

4. As students are ready to transition to writing, provide them with copies of a supportive structure such as the one that follows so they can write out their If I Were the Author reflections.

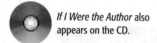

If I Were the Author also appears on the CD.

Striving readers benefit from opportunities to take a critical stance and analyze the selections they read.

If I Were the Author

Reader/Responder: _____ Date: _____

Book Title and Author: _____

Things about this book/story that I would be proud to say I created (illustrations, character descriptions, beginning, ending, and so on).

_____

_____

I would be proud of these story elements because _____

_____

Things about this book/story that I would change _____

_____

I would change this because _____

_____

My rating for this story:

This is the most amazing story   I wasn't very
I have ever read   fond of it

10   9   8   7   6   5   4   3   2   1   0

I selected this rating because _____

_____

Small Group

Partners

Memorable Moments

This *solution*, Memorable Moments, helps striving readers acknowledge that all readers have moments when they connect strongly to a reading selection. This helps them to understand the role that their personal preferences and background knowledge play in building understanding. The goal is to help striving readers share their observations about points in the text that were most meaningful to them and why.

Memorable Moments helps striving readers understand that each individual reader has unique connections to a story.

Steps for *Memorable Moments*

1. In a small group setting, use a familiar text to model how you reflect back on the selection and mark points in the text that you found to be memorable. With striving readers observing closely, turn back through the pages of a book and place sticky notes at the point in the story that you found to be "memorable." With each, explain why that event or situation captured your interest.

2. Extend understanding by thinking aloud about your most memorable moment in the entire book. Then, share a quote as an example of how the author created the memorable moment.

3. Provide readers with an opportunity to reconnect with a book that they particularly enjoyed, following the process you demonstrated and marking "memorable" points with sticky notes.

4. Invite partners to share their Memorable Moments with each other, even if they selected different books. Coach and support them to provide reasons why that point in the text was important to them.

Memorable Moments also appears on the CD.

Spirited dialogue and personal connections make Memorable Moments a sure winner with striving readers.

5. Present your students with a framework such as the one that follows so they can turn their powerful connections into a piece of writing.

Memorable Moments

Reader: _____ Selection: _____ Date: _____

Before I read the story, I anticipated a memorable moment would be _____

_____

_____

_____

As I read, the memorable moments that most captured my attention and interest were _____

_____

_____

_____

As I finished the story, the overall most memorable moment was _____

_____

_____

_____

I have selected the following quote as an example of how the author created the memorable moment:

_____

_____

_____

Underlying Principles

- **Structured story retelling** relates to increased comprehension and vocabulary acquisition among English language learners, special education students, and children of poverty (de Quiros and Migdalia 2008; Duke and Pearson 2002; Vaughn and Gersten 2000).

- **Reading comprehension must be taught explicitly** from the primary grades and on into high school (Snow 2002).

- **Comprehension can be improved** by activating background knowledge, providing graphic organizers, focusing on key concepts and vocabulary, and engaging learners in pre- and postwriting activities (Pearson 2008; Allington 2009; Pressley 2002).

- **Readers use** metacognitive strategies as they read. Those strategies include: monitoring for meaning, using and creating schema, asking questions, determining importance, inferring, using sensory and emotional images, and synthesizing (Keene and Zimmerman 2007).

- **Effective teachers** ask higher-level questions that require students to infer, think beyond the text, and make connections to other texts and their lives (Schwartz 2006; Short and Fitzsimmons 2007; Taberski 2011).

- **The reciprocal relationship** between reading and writing is well established, especially in terms of composing and comprehension (Vaughn et al. 2000; Allington 2006; Cummins 2009).

- **PET scans indicate** that passive word-calling is associated with low levels of metabolic brain activity. The greatest brain activation occurred when readers were told that they would be retelling the story they were reading to someone else (Willis 2007).

- **Meaning continually evolves** as readers respond to the inner dialogue with a text (Au 2010; Cooper, Char, and Kieger 2006; Harvey and Daniels 2009).

- **Dramatic enactments** activate psychomotor memory, increase content retention, and deepen comprehension (Gill 2008; Jensen 2008; Wilhelm 1997; Willis 2007; Vaughn and Linan-Thompson 2004).

- **Culturally responsive instruction** scaffolds understanding and access (Au 2010; Gay 2000; Knapp 2007).

PART THREE

Solutions for Assessment

PART

3

Solutions for Assessment

Formative assessment is a process used by teachers and students as a natural part of instruction. With formative assessment, classroom teachers and interventionists engage in close observation of individual learners, gathering data that can be used to adjust ongoing teaching and learning. This close observation and collection of evidence inform and reshape instruction so it matches specific learner needs— improving students' achievement of intended instructional outcomes. This process is the heart of accelerated learning for striving readers.

–L. Hoyt

Formative assessment, an essential component for accelerating the learning of striving readers, is meant to occur within the natural contexts of teaching and learning—within a classroom or specialty environment. During a learning experience, the teacher closely observes learners—noting the strategies

Olympic judges learn to analyze and place numerical values on the performances of athletes. Highly qualified teachers are capable of the same level of expert analyses as they support striving learners.

striving readers are employing, assessing the success of their efforts, and noting progress since the last observation (Barrentine and Stokes 2005; Bender 2002; Coffey 2009). Sometimes data are gathered within the context of whole-class instruction as students interact with partners, learning teams, or an independent task. Sometimes data are gathered in the more intimate settings provided by small-group instruction or individual conferences. Other times, artifacts and writing samples are gathered after a learning event to enable reflective and focused analysis of learning. Learning artifacts and writing samples enable a reflective teacher to identify points of progress, highlight areas of need, or collect a tangible record of learning accomplishments.

It is vital that these opportunities for data gathering and close observation offer information about the full spectrum of behaviors that comprise effective, thoughtful reading. Focusing on a single subsystem of literacy such as fluency or word study can offer a dangerously limited view of reader development and could limit a striving reader's ability to achieve the complex literacies that are demanded by future schooling and the workplace—and that are endorsed by the Common Core Curriculum Standards (2010). Anecdotal notes, work samples, rubrics, checklists, and self-reflections work together to offer a broad view of learner development and empower classroom teachers and interventionists to make the best possible decisions about instruction.

We often hear of schools and districts that select an assessment based on how rapidly it can be administered or how quickly the tool generates numerical values. However, it is essential to recognize that while many available measures do produce data quickly, they are often measuring dimensions of reading that are not directly linked to high levels of reading competence. As we consider data gathering options and the ultimate goal of informing instruction, it is helpful to remember that some behaviors that can be measured are not worth measuring. And there are some understandings that, while not easily measured, are fundamentally important to reader development. Jane Olson, one of the authors of this resource, uses the analogy of an Olympic athlete. She reminds us that a swimmer's speed can be measured to the hundredth of a second; a shot-putter's distance can be measured to the nearest centimeter; but a gymnast's technique and stylized performance can't be measured in those terms. You can't measure the artful line of an arm extended in flight, but the technicality and beauty of the move can be *judged* or *assessed*. Judging based on solid criteria can be valid, reliable, and focused when there is a high degree of inter-rater reliability. Olympic judges learn to analyze and place numerical values on the performances of athletes. Highly qualified teachers are capable of the same level of expert analyses.

With next steps in instruction as the central focus, close observation and formative assessments guide teacher decision making and instructional planning so instruction and learner need are inextricably tied together. This places observable behaviors as the driving force in teacher decision making, coaching, and lesson planning—guiding teachers who observe closely to design instruction with the greatest potential of lifting learner performance. Close observation of individuals as they operate within a range of grouping patterns and learning contexts is essential to responsive lesson design and accelerated achievement. As you noticed in Part 1 and Part 2 of this resource, *solutions* suggested in the Side-by-Side feature were based on close observation and data. This elevates instruction to a higher level as the instruction is informed by data on each individual learner.

There is no program that can engage in close observation as a striving learner navigates a leveled reading selection. There is no standardized test that can analyze the phonic knowledge that is applied as an emergent writer laboriously constructs a written sentence. There is no outside force that can substitute for a teacher who listens closely as a language learner applies academic vocabulary and engages in a peer conversation. This ability to closely observe, notice nuances in learning behavior, then respond with instruction that is targeted to learner need separates teachers who make exceptional progress with striving students from teachers who do not (Marzano 2006).

With formative assessment, every instructional moment provides opportunity for close observation of students:

- Observe how well striving readers are attending to and applying demonstrated strategies.

- Notice and record reading behaviors that help striving readers attain meaning or to unlock word parts.

- Attend to patterns in reader development and think toward next steps in instruction.

- Record expansion of oral language or integrated use of academic vocabulary.

- Document a striving reader's ability to reflect on content and offer critical, analytical reflections.
- Analyze writing samples for evidence of content understanding, sentence structure, grammar use, and word choice.

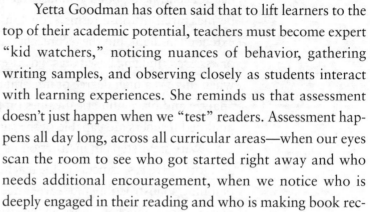

Yetta Goodman has often said that to lift learners to the top of their academic potential, teachers must become expert "kid watchers," noticing nuances of behavior, gathering writing samples, and observing closely as students interact with learning experiences. She reminds us that assessment doesn't just happen when we "test" readers. Assessment happens all day long, across all curricular areas—when our eyes scan the room to see who got started right away and who needs additional encouragement, when we notice who is deeply engaged in their reading and who is making book recommendations to friends. When we notice the kinds of books striving readers are choosing, gather them close to hear them read, or listen closely to conversations as they share their learning with a partner—we are demonstrating close observation and kid watching (Wilde 1996).

The following assessments are selected to help you create a broad view of reader development—observing the wide range of understandings that are essential to helping striving students grow into mature and confident readers. We encourage you to try out a range of assessment tools to find those that best suit your personal style and the needs of the students you serve. With close observation and data, you will be able to make the most informed decisions possible from the learning experiences offered in this resource. It is not our intent that the formative assessments presented here be used as activities. Rather, we hope that you approach possible *solutions* with a diagnostic stance—choosing those that best support and link to the observations and data you have collected for each striving reader.

The forms that follow are all available on the CD-ROM for ease of printing. We also encourage you to personalize the *assessment solutions* by adjusting and modifying the forms to ensure that you have data-gathering tools that match your own personal style and the needs of the striving readers you serve.

Finally, as you engage in close observation, we encourage you to give striving readers opportunities for self-assessment and reflection—directing their attention to their strengths as well as their learning goals. One of the greatest gifts we can offer striving readers is to help them identify which reading behaviors they are already using that are helpful and should be repeated. Striving readers hear all too often about their weaknesses. If we, as their coaches and mentors, can celebrate their strengths in concert with teaching new and effective approaches for engaging with print, striving readers can move forward to integrate new learning.

Close observation and note taking as striving readers are engaged with learning provide assessment and inform instruction. Notice the teacher on the right of this photo recording observational notes on her clipboard.

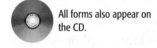

All forms also appear on the CD.

Collect Data on a Broad Spectrum of Reading Behaviors

The *Ongoing Broad-Spectrum Profile* also appears on the CD.

Ongoing Broad-Spectrum Profile

The following *assessment solution* is designed to serve as a record-keeping tool for monitoring progress across the full spectrum of effective reader behaviors you may be tracking for striving readers. By monitoring a broad base of reading understandings for your striving readers, you can easily track progress, target lessons to match needs, or share data with a colleague or parent.

This tool can also be used as a summary sheet for the checklists, anecdotal notes, rubrics, and learning artifacts that you may have collected for individual learners.

The following chart has sample data to demonstrate how the Ongoing Broad-Spectrum Profile might be used.

Ongoing Broad-Spectrum Profile

Reader name: *Selina* Data collection and analysis by: *Mrs. Davis, Mrs. Olson, Mrs. Boswell*

	Reading Level	Accuracy	Balance of Cueing Systems (meaning, structure, visual)	Use of Fix-Up Strategies	Comprehension Observations/ Data Nonfiction	Comprehension Observations/ Data Fiction	Oral Language	Expressive Oral Reading	Word-Solving Strategies	Written Response to Reading
Data Point 1 Date *9/22*	D	92%	Heavily dependent on visual cues.	Uses picture cues. Occasionally backtracks.	Needs a lot of support with concepts and vocabulary.	Identifies with characters. Needs support with problem–solution structure.	Uses short sentences and phrases in oral communication.	2 points on scoring guide.	Uses beginning and ending sounds.	Responds with labeled drawings
Data Point 2 Date *10/6*	F	95%	Better integration of meaning cues. Most sentences make sense.	Back-tracking and questioning to self-monitor understanding.	Growing in ability to integrate prior knowledge.	Has problem–solution structure. Needs to notice event sequences.	Interpersonal communications becoming more complex. Using content-specific vocabulary to talk about learning.	4 points on scoring guide.	Chunks words and uses analogy.	Offers opinions. I like it. It was good.

Analysis *There is progress in all areas. In particular, there is growth in the use of academic vocabulary, fluency, and the use of fix-up strategies.*

Next Steps *Classroom teacher and specialists will concentrate on trying to lift Selina into level G books with 95% accuracy and solid comprehension. She will self-assess her fix-up strategy use after each small-group experience as well as independent reading. Emphasis will be placed on nonfiction to empower her content understanding and build academic vocabulary.*

Ongoing Broad-Spectrum Profile

Reader name _____ Data collection and analysis by _____

	Reading Level	Accuracy	Balance of Cueing Systems (meaning, structure, visual)	Use of Fix-Up Strategies	Comprehension Observations/Data		Oral Language	Expressive Oral Reading	Word-Solving Strategies	Written Response to Reading
					Nonfiction	Fiction				
Data Point 1 Date										
Data Point 2 Date										
Analysis										
Next Steps										
Data Point 3 Date										
Data Point 4 Date										
Analysis										
Next Steps										
Data Point 5 Date										
Data Point 6 Date										
Analysis										
Next Steps										

The *Individual Conference Notes* also
appears on the CD.

Individual Conferences

An individual conference is an *assessment solution* that takes the form of a personal meeting between a teacher and a striving reader. During this time, a teacher might guide a striving reader to:

- talk about what she is reading

- read a passage while the teacher takes an oral reading record and checks for expressive oral reading

- list the different ways to approach a challenging word

- provide a retell of a text as the teacher analyzes and completes a retell scoring guide

- focus on text structure with a graphic organizer

- offer critical, analytical, or evaluative observations about the selection

Within this context of personal attention and partnership, a mentor or coach can identify and celebrate something a striving reader is doing well by pointing out a reading behavior that is being used effectively. Then, a teaching point is selected and this personal moment is used as an opportunity to explicitly demonstrate a new understanding that will support reading growth.

It helps to sit side by side—in a position of partnership. This position makes it possible for teacher and student to see the book clearly, which is important for data collection.

Anecdotal Notes

Anecdotal notes are brief reflections or observational notes about reader behavior or reminders about next steps in instruction. Through these notes, teachers can document a striving reader's use of meaning-seeking behaviors, linguistic competency, decoding skills, comprehension moves, and fix-up strategies. The notes can also be used to record a student's choice of text and level of fluency and whether a child is self-monitoring for meaning.

Individual conference notes are a collection site for anecdotal observations, reading-level designations, and "next steps" for instruction.

Individual Conference Notes			
Name			
Date	**Observations** *What strategies did I notice the child using independently?*	**Teaching Point** *What strategy did I teach the reader in today's conference?*	**What's Next** *What are the next steps for this reader?*
Oct. 2 A Frog Has A Sticky Tongue, Level F	- Looks at picture clues. - Uses headings - Backtracking to maintain meaning. - Strong retell today. - Over-reliant on phonics.	- Think about what makes sense then use the beginning and ending sounds.	- Self-reflection on meaning - Graphic organizer to support meaning while reading.
Oct. 6 How Do Frogs Grow, Level G	- Predicts words that make sense and start with the same letter. - Nice fluency today	- Word prediction. List words you expect to see on this page.	Key word strategy

Although there are many ways to collect anecdotal notes, you might consider using:

- a template like the one shown to collect your anecdotal notes

- address labels such as those made for computers that you carry with you as you confer with each student (Once you have recorded your observations, the labels can be peeled off and placed on a form that you have prepared—one for each child.)

- a spiral-bound notebook

- composition book

- three-ring binder with a tab for each striving reader

These observational notes create a history for each reader and provide the teacher with a wealth of information about reading behaviors that can be interpreted and analyzed when planning for instruction.

Although one-to-one conferences are a perfect vehicle for anecdotal notes, keep in mind that observations during independent reading, guided reading, partner reading, and small-group discussions throughout the instructional day are also rich sources of information that can be added to anecdotal notes.

Anecdotal notes capture observations of learner behavior and focus on next steps in instruction.

Individual Conference Notes

Name of Reader _____

Date and Text	Observations What strategies did I notice this reader using independently?	Teaching Point What strategy did I explicitly demonstrate for the reader in today's conference?	What's Next What are the next steps for this reader?

Conferring Log: Comprehension

A Conferring Log is an *assessment solution* that enables teachers to document and examine the kinds of comprehension strategies striving readers are utilizing as they engage with text over time. Its power is the data that are collected, allowing a teacher to analyze which strategies the student is using with multiple texts—demonstrating transfer of strategy use. Longitudinal data collection such as this enables a teacher to identify which strategies require further instruction and which are fully implemented in a wide range of texts and to document whether strategy use is persistent in both fiction and nonfiction selections. Different from anecdotal notes, in which information is collected in narrative form, this form collects data with simple tally marks so frequency of strategy use can be noted and compared.

The Conferring Log example that follows provides an example of the kinds of data that can be gathered over time during individual conferences. Most importantly, notice the Notes and Next Steps for Instruction section. This is the link that makes the data meaningful as striving readers have little to gain if their reading data are collected and then ignored. The secret is to use data to inform and shape instruction.

Conferring Log: Comprehension

Student			Grade											
			Behaviors Observed by Teacher											
Reading Conference (Date)	Text and Genre	Student Response: What did you do to help yourself understand this section? (Record Student Response)	Use Fix-Up Strategies					Create Sensory Images	Determine Importance	Infer or Predict	Question	Make Connections	Summarize (Rate 1–5)	**Notes and Next Steps for Instruction**
			Backtrack	Read On	Use Beginning and Ending Sounds	Chunk	Use Picture Clues							
9/28	Green Wilma (F)	Looked at pictures and asked myself questions	////	///		/	//			/	//	/	4	Focus on determining importance
9/30	Frogs, Frogs, Frogs! (NF)	Thought about another book about frogs that was read previously				//	///	/	//		//	//	5	Chunking cold-blood-ed trop-i-cal *Work on rereading to check facts

Conferring Log: Comprehension

Student · **Grade**

Reading Conference (Date)	Text and Genre	Student Response: What did you do to help yourself understand this section? (Record Student Response)	Behaviors Observed by Teacher											Notes and Next Steps for Instruction
			Use Fix-Up Strategies					Create Sensory Images	Determine Importance	Infer or Predict	Question	Make Connections	Summarize (Rate 1–5)	
			Backtrack	Read On	Use Beginning and Ending Sounds	Chunk	Use Picture Clues							

Self-Monitoring Strategy Scoring Guide

The Strategy Scoring Guide is an *assessment solution* designed to help teachers gather quick, informal data that can help them monitor and support a striving reader's use of reading strategies.

Consider collecting this information during the natural course of the day. You can ask a student to read from a self-selected text during independent reading, from an assigned selection during small group instruction, or from an accessible text utilized during science or social studies. Recording data over time and in multiple contexts will help you to notice patterns of strategy use that can inform your instructional planning.

Here's an example:

Self-Monitoring Strategy Scoring Guide   Reader: *Emilio*

	Date Observation 1	Date Observation 2	Date Observation 3	Date Observation 4	Date Observation 5	Date Observation 6
Text	*9/04* *Bats*	*9/20 Nocturnal* *Animals*	*10/4* *Tornado*			
Level	*E*	*F*	*G*			
Fiction or Nonfiction	*NF*	*NF*	*NF*			
Strategy Scoring Guide Rating	*Emergent*	*Developing*	*Developing*			
Strengths	*Picture Clues,* *Word Parts*	*Self-* *Questioning,* *Read-On*	*Sum Up*			
Instructional Implications: Support Needed	*Self-* *Questioning,* *Re-reading*	*Pause to* *Sum Up*	*Shift Rate*			

Self-Monitoring Strategy Scoring Guide   Reader: _____

	Date Observation 1	Date Observation 2	Date Observation 3	Date Observation 4	Date Observation 5	Date Observation 6
Text						
Level						
Fiction or Nonfiction						
Strategy Scoring Guide Rating						
Strengths						
Instructional Implications: Support Needed						

Key to scoring:

Proficient: Eight to ten self-monitoring strategies

Developing: Three to seven self-monitoring strategies

Emergent: One to two self-monitoring strategies

Date behaviors as they appear.

_____ picture clues	_____ re-reading
_____ graphic supports such as charts and bold print	_____ reading on for more context
_____ shifts in reading speed to respond to the text	_____ analysis of word parts
_____ self-questioning before and during reading	_____ synthesizing of information
_____ making connections to prior knowledge	_____ pause to sum up

Collect Data with Observational Checklists

Observational Checklists I and II appear full size on the CD.

Observational Checklist

The Observational Checklist is composed of questions that are designed to help teachers collect data on a variety of emergent and early reading behaviors. These data can be collected through close observation during small-group instruction, partner reading, or individual reading conferences. We find it is helpful to record dates when the target behavior appears and then confirm that this striving reader is using the behavior across many different texts and text types. It is also helpful to consider adding a check mark when you provide direct instruction in a behavior so you can remember to recheck that strategy in a few days.

Once you have completed your preliminary data collection using the observational checklist, you can decide which areas would benefit from further assessment and analysis. The goal is to record reader development over time.

Observational Checklist I

Reader _____

Dates Behavior Observed
Key: F (fiction), NF (nonfiction)
✓ (provided instruction on this behavior)
+ (behavior in place)

Behaviors Observation	Observation 1	Observation 2	Observation 3	Observation 4	Observation 5
Is the reader matching voice to print? Saying one word for each word on the page?					
Is the reader integrating high-frequency (sight) words without attempting to sound them out?					
Do the reader's miscues make sense (meaning cues)?					
Do the miscues sound right grammatically: a noun for a noun, verb for a verb, etc. (syntactic cues)?					
Are the miscues visually similar; for example, does the child insert *house* for *horse* or *nine* for *none* (visual cues)?					
Is the reader starting the word correctly, but guessing at the end?					
Is the reader able to break challenging words into chunks that support decoding?					
Is the reader able to use analogy and think of words that are similar to one that is presenting a challenge?					
Is the reader hesitating after making a miscue, realizing that it may not make sense?					
Does the reader employ fix-up strategies when she encounters difficulty?					
Does the reader attempt multiple strategies when encountering difficulty? • Reread • Read on • Get started with the first letter • Take the word apart • Think of another word like the tricky word (analogy) • Run finger under the word and say sounds slowly					

Observational Checklist II

Reader _____

Dates Behavior Observed
Key: F (fiction), NF (nonfiction)
✓ (provided instruction on this behavior)
+ (behavior in place)

Behaviors Observation	Observation 1	Observation 2	Observation 3	Observation 4	Observation 5
Does the reader read in phrases, with expression, at a rate appropriate to the text?					
Does the reader cross-check with visual information: pictures, diagrams, labels, headings?					
Does the reader give a complete retelling of fiction: characters, setting, events, problem–solution?					
Does the reader give a complete retelling of nonfiction: main ideas, supporting details, statement of importance?					
Is the reader able to independently select books that are comfortable and comprehensible reading?					
Does the reader choose a variety of genres, balancing fiction and nonfiction?					
Is the reader demonstrating stamina and the ability to attend to text when reading independently? For how many minutes can the reader sustain attention?					
What comprehension strategies were evident in today's conference? Mark a + for strategies applied independently. Mark a ✓ for strategies applied with coaching or probing.					
• Self-monitoring					
• Making connections					
• Summarizing					
• Questioning					
• Inferring and predicting					
• Visualizing					

*Look Closely
at Miscues*

Oral Reading Record and *Reading
Profile* also appear on the CD.

Analyzing Miscues

*From the time a child tries to retell a story from the pictures in
a book until the reader has become a silent reader, [analyses of
miscues taken at selected intervals] can plot a path of progress.*

—Marie Clay, *An Observation Survey of Early Literacy Achievement*

Analyses of miscues, often known as oral reading records or running
records, are highly important tools as they allow us to closely examine the
way that a striving reader interacts with a text—noticing reading behaviors
such as repetitions, omissions, accuracy, appeals for assistance, and so on.
They also allow us to determine, through an analysis of accuracy, a student's reading level.

With *assessment solutions* such as those that follow, closely observing
teachers focused on striving readers collect and analyze reading miscues
every week to monitor progress and assess the appropriateness of reading
material. Most importantly, analyses of miscues allow us to analyze in
detail the processing that readers do as they navigate text (Goodman 1969;
Goodman, Watson, and Burke 2005; Clay 2002).

Like a traditional IRI (individual reading
inventory), oral reading records identify points
where a striving reader reads accurately (a
check mark) or deviates from the printed text
by omitting a word or substituting a word that
is different from the one in print.

What differentiates an oral reading
record from an IRI is that you don't just count
errors and check accuracy. Instead, the close
observer asks, *Why did the reader make that
miscue? Was he using meaning and trying to
make sense (using meaning cues)? Was he trying to think of another word that looks like
the one in the sentence and selected one that
visually looks a lot the same (using visual
cues)? Was the reader trying to use what he
knows about grammar and word order and
inserting a structurally similar word—a noun for a noun or a verb for a
verb (using cues related to language structure)?* By analyzing *why*, instead
of simply checking for accuracy, a close observer gains powerful insights
into the reading behavior of a striving reader. The key shown here shows
possible codes that may be utilized.

Key

✓	word read correctly
(word)	word omitted
house / horse	substitution
a—	child only produced the beginning sound
s/c	self-correction
R	repetition of word
/	pause
A	appeals to teacher for help

An example: If a reader said *house* instead of *horse* in a sentence about horseback riding, it is clear that the reader is using visual cues—thinking about the way the word looks. The reader is also using structural cues as *house* and *horse* are both nouns. The reader is not using meaning as *riding a house* makes no sense at all. To record this analysis, you might show the following:

Substitution	What cues was the reader using?		
	Meaning	Structure	Visual
house / horse	—	✓	✓

Although there are any number of forms, formats, and coding systems for oral reading records, there is no one correct way to gather the data and analyze it. What is important is that a mentor/coach looks beyond accuracy to analyze which cues a striving reader is using so the reader can be supported in learning to utilize the full range of cues—meaning, structure, and visual.

The two forms that follow on pages 159 and 160—the Oral Reading Record and the Reading Profile—will help you engage in analysis of miscues. What separates them is that the Oral Reading Record on page 159 looks deeply at a reader's interaction with a single text. It provides an opportunity to notice omissions, backtracking, repeated words, and so on. In contrast, the Reading Profile on page 160 focuses on substitutions and is designed to look at patterns over time. With the Reading Profile, you may gather a substitution during independent reading, two more during science, and a few additional substitutions during small-group instruction. When you have ten substitutions, you are ready to analyze the cues used and plot the information into the bar graph at the top of the page. This graph provides a powerful visual tool as you converse with colleagues and parents about the needs of striving readers.

Running records or oral reading records, designed by Marie Clay and based on the work of Ken and Yetta Goodman, offer powerful insights into why readers are making errors. The analysis of the closely observing teacher guides instruction so striving readers receive support in utilizing meaning, visual, and structural cues.

Oral Reading Record

Name _____ Date _____

Observing Teacher _____

Text Title _____ Text Level _____

Accuracy rate: words read correctly divided by total number of words = _____%

Page #	Accuracy — Record (✓) for words read accurately. Show substitutions by writing the substitution (a word or partial word) over the top of the word in the text. Show omissions by circling the omitted word.	Number of Miscues on the Page	Number of Self-Corrections on the Page	Examine Cues Used: Analyze and Wonder: Which Cues Did the Reader Use?			Observations About Self-Monitoring and Fix-Up Strategies
				Meaning	Structure	Visual	

Analysis:

• Note use of cues (meaning, visual, structure)

_____

• Note use of fix-up strategies: read on, backtrack, use beginning sounds, picture clues, etc.)

_____

• Note use of expressive oral reading (phrasing, expression), match of rate to text and purpose

Reading Profile

Student _____ Date _____ Text _____

Substitution Comparison

Miscues	The Student Read	The Text Says	Meaning	Structure	Visual	Self-Correct
1						
2						
3						
4						
5						
6						
7						
8						
9						
10						
Total						

Counts of Strategy Use
(Tally or comment)

Meaning (Semantic Cues)

"Does it make sense?" _____

Reads on _____

Backtracks _____

Self-corrects _____

Meaningful substitutions _____

Picture clues_____

Structure (Syntactic Cues)

*"Does it sound right?"*_____

Use grammar _____

Word order _____

Noun/verb agreement _____

Visual (Grapho-Phonic Cues)

"Does it look right?" _____

Uses beginning sounds _____

Ending sounds _____

Chunks words _____

Cueing System Percentages

	Meaning	Structure	Visual	Self-Correct
100				
90				
80				
70				
60				
50				
40				
30				
20				
10				

Implications for Instruction

From Linda Hoyt, Snapshots, © 2000. Portsmouth, NH: Heinemann. Used with permission. May be photocopied for classroom use only.

*Gather Data
on Strategy Use
over Time*

Observation of Reading Strategies and
Strategic Behaviors Checklists I and *II*
also appear on the CD.

Reading Strategy Observations and Checklists

As is true of the *assessment solutions* on the preceding pages, the following tools offer a range of possibility for data collection. You may find a single tool that will work well for all of your students or select observation and data collection tools that match the individual needs of the striving readers that you support.

The Observation of Reading Strategies on page 162 provides a structured scaffold for close observation of four different texts with the same reader. These observations do not need to occur on the same day. The data can easily be collected over time and in differing kinds of reading selections.

The Strategic Behaviors Checklists I and II on pages 163 and 164 present scaffolds for close observation of striving readers at differing levels of development in a single setting. The Strategic Behaviors Checklist I is designed for emergent and developing readers. The Strategic Behaviors Checklist II is structured to support striving readers who are ready for more sophisticated levels of interpretation and analysis.

The Informational Strategy Checklist on page 166 provides important information on the strategies that are specific to reading a nonfiction selection. Knowing that nonfiction reading comprises up to 95 percent of the reading done by the average American adult, this genre is particularly important to striving readers and should be monitored closely.

The Self-Reflection of Strategy Use and Personal Reading Assessment on pages 167 and 168 are designed to engage striving readers in self-assessment and reflection—a vitally important metacognitive step that will enhance self-efficacy and independence of strategy use.

Observation of Reading Strategies

Reader _____ Observing Teacher _____

	Text #1	Text #2	Text #3	Text #4
Title				
Level				
Date				
The reader				
Is able to predict words based on a picture preview				
Uses pictures to think about meaning				
Thinks about experiences that may be connected to this text				
Uses beginning and ending sounds				
Chunks words				
Matches voice to print				
Uses context clues				
Backtracks when the meaning isn't clear				
Looks for little words in big words				
Stops frequently to do a mini-retell of what has been read				
Consciously tries to remember important ideas				
Makes connections				
Tries to visualize				
Thinks of questions about the topic				
Observations about this reader in this text				
Implications for instruction				

Strategic Behaviors Checklist I

Reader _____ Date _____

Text _____ Level _____ Observing Teacher _____

While previewing the text, the reader:

(   ) Holds the book correctly

(   ) Knows where to begin

(   ) Knows how to turn the pages in sequence

(   ) Attends closely to photographs and illustrations

(   ) Asks questions or makes comments while surveying visuals

(   ) Shares connections to experiences, other books on the topic, or other sources of information on this topic

While reading the text, the reader:

(   ) Tracks the print from left to right, top to bottom

(   ) Uses picture clues for clues to meaning

(   ) Matches voice to print

(   ) Recognizes when the reading does not make sense

(   ) Backtracks to reread for meaning and fluency

(   ) Uses beginning and ending sounds

(   ) Chunks words

(   ) Uses context clues

(   ) Asks questions about the content

After reading, the reader:

(   ) Provides a clear and well-organized retell

(   ) Includes important ideas

(   ) Adds supporting details

(   ) Includes an opinion or evaluative statement about the text

Strengths of this reader: _____

_____

Next steps for instruction: _____

_____

Strategic Behaviors Checklist II

Name of Reader _____ Date _____ Text Selection/Level _____

Rating completed by

( ) Reader: Read a passage quietly to yourself and focus on these behaviors.

( ) Observing teacher: As the student reads, observe closely and notice which behaviors are in place.

Reading Strategy Use	Clearly Used				Not Used

Before reading

Previewed text before reading	5	4	3	2	1
Consciously activated prior knowledge	5	4	3	2	1
Predicted words likely to appear in the text	5	4	3	2	1
Established personal questions for reading	5	4	3	2	1

During reading

Dealt with challenges in text by:

Reading on to gain context	5	4	3	2	1
Backtracking to regain momentum or check a fact	5	4	3	2	1
Chunking unknown words	5	4	3	2	1
Using context clues for unknown words	5	4	3	2	1
Self-correcting	5	4	3	2	1
Reads with rate appropriate to the text	5	4	3	2	1

After reading

Uses the text to support and clarify points	5	4	3	2	1
Identifies main ideas	5	4	3	2	1
Makes inferences beyond the text	5	4	3	2	1
Makes connections	5	4	3	2	1
Refers to the author's craft	5	4	3	2	1
Makes critical/evaluative statements	5	4	3	2	1
Questions the author's choices of words, organization, visual supports, clarity of communication	5	4	3	2	1
Communicates with others to explore understanding	5	4	3	2	1

Particular strengths of this reader: _____

Goals and instructional focus points needed for this reader: _____

Informational Text Strategy Observation

A Nonfiction Strategy Checklist is an *assessment solution* that allows mentors and coaches to closely observe and record the behaviors that striving readers utilize when engaging with nonfiction selections.

Before Reading

Provide the student with an unfamiliar text, written at the reader's independent reading level. As you closely observe this prereading interaction with the text, pay close attention to what the reader does first. Does she automatically preview the text, as good readers of nonfiction do? Hopefully, she begins by looking closely at visuals such as photographs, diagrams, charts, or graphs. It should also be clear if the reader is skimming the table of contents and headings to get an idea of key points that will be made in the book. A probing question you might ask during this prereading observation is: *Based on your preview of this selection, what words do you expect to encounter in this book?*

During Reading

As the student begins to read, take note of the strategies he employs. Does he take time to connect to the photographs and read the captions? Does he use the information from the visuals to help him make sense of the written text? Place a check mark next to the strategies that you see the reader use.

When the student has read the text, or a portion of the text, ask him to briefly summarize what he has read so far. Is he able to recall the main idea and include some supporting details?

After Reading

Consider asking the reader a question or two that would require her to use the table of contents or the index such as: *If you were to quickly return to the section on _____, what page would you turn to?*

Then, ask her opinion about a theme or concept from the text and ask her to find evidence to back up her opinion.

Continue recording observations on the checklist, noting points where instruction is needed to ensure that this reader becomes comfortable with a wide range of navigational strategies for nonfiction.

Informational Text Strategy Observation

Name _____

Date _____

Text read _____ Level _____

	Informational Strategy Checklist	Observations and Implications for Instruction
(✓)	**Before reading**	
	Previews text before reading	
	Uses illustrations, photos, and title to make predictions	
	Generates questions before reading	
	Refers to the table of contents or index	
	Is able to predict words that are likely to appear in the text	
(✓)	**During reading**	
	Visualizes while reading	
	Makes inferences	
	Pauses to use pictures, graphs, captions, and other text features	
	May refer to the glossary to check a term	
	Generates during-reading questions	
	Varies reading rate to match the demands of the text	
(✓)	**After reading**	
	When asked, can find evidence in text to support opinions	
	Can summarize the main ideas and can include supporting details	
	Synthesizes information from both the text and the visuals	
	Uses the index or table of contents to satisfy a question or support an opinion with evidence	
	Generates after-reading questions	
	Rereads to check a fact or confirm understanding	

L. Hoyt, K. Davis, J. Olson, and K. Boswell, Solutions for Reading Comprehension, © 2011. Portsmouth, NH: Heinemann. May be photocopied for classroom use only.

Self-Reflection of Strategy Use

Name _____

Date _____

Before reading, I

____ look at the title and the pictures

____ think about the topic and what I already know

____ predict words that I think are likely to appear

During reading, I

____ look for the words that I thought would appear

____ get a mental picture in my head

____ make connections to what I already know

____ use fix-up strategies on tricky words

- think about what makes sense

- check the picture

- look at the beginning sounds

- use word parts

- backtrack and reread

- put in another word that makes sense

After reading, I

____ pull it all together in my head and think about the important parts

____ ask questions

____ pick my favorite parts

Personal Reading Assessment

Reader _____ Date _____

Some books I have read and enjoyed: _____

_____

I am learning how to be a good reader. One important thing I have learned is _____

_____.

A new reading strategy I have learned is _____. I tried it when

I was reading _____ and I noticed that _____.

My favorite book is _____. I liked it because _____.

While I was reading this book, I used the strategy of _____. It helped me

because _____

_____.

Some other strategies I know how to use are: _____

_____

_____

Adapted from Linda Hoyt, Make It Real, © 2002. Portsmouth, NH: Heinemann. Used with permission. May be photocopied for classroom use only.

Nonfiction Strategy: Self-Reflection

Reader _____ Text _____

Today while reading a nonfiction selection, I remembered to:

Utilize the table of contents	Yes	No
Skim quickly before reading to get the big idea	Yes	No
Look for key words	Yes	No
Read the headings	Yes	No
Use photographs, illustrations, charts, and graphs	Yes	No
Think of questions		
Before reading	Yes	No
During reading	Yes	No
After reading	Yes	No
Sometimes skim a paragraph and then go back to read it slowly for details	Yes	No
Use the index	Yes	No
Pause often to think about what I am learning	Yes	No
Try to visualize as I read	Yes	No

While I was reading, I understood best when I _____

_____.

Next time I read for information, I am going to be sure to _____

_____.

Adapted from Linda Hoyt, Make It Real, *© 2002. Portsmouth, NH: Heinemann. Used with permission. May be photocopied for classroom use only.*

Observation of Oral Language

An Observation of Oral Language checklist is an *assessment solution* that allows a teacher to observe and record nuances of oral language development, over time. These data can be collected when listening to a student during partner conversations or small-group discussions. The observing teacher might also gather data while coaching the student one-on-one during independent reading.

As you notice an oral language behavior, simply denote the date the behavior was observed. Over time, it will become clear which oral language behaviors are in place for the student and which would benefit from further modeling and support.

Please note that the language competencies on the checklist are not intended as qualifying or exit criteria from a program for those learning English as an additional language. These are language competencies that support all striving learners in developing a strong base of linguistic competence.

Observation of Oral Language

Learner _____ Grade _____

	Date Observed	Date Observed	Date Observed	Date Observed
Responds to simple questions				
Knows the difference between a question and a statement				
Can express an opinion				
Asks for clarification when he or she doesn't understand				
Can retell a personal experience (includes *who, what, where, when*)				
Shifts language to match social setting (e.g., talking with friends vs. talking with principal)				
Can express past tense				
Uses language of future tense (e.g., When will we get to do that?)				
Can differentiate between singular and plural				
Speaks in complete sentences				
Notices when language is grammatically incorrect and tries again				
Participates in social conversation, taking turns as a speaker and listener				
Participates in partner and small-group conversations about content, using topic-specific vocabulary				
Uses language of concepts that are not concrete such as *love, hope, wish, what if*, etc.				
Uses literary language (e.g., *once upon a time, character, setting, problem, solution*)				
Understands many prepositions (*in, out, under, through*, etc.)				
Uses connectives (*because, if, after, next, finally*)				
Makes connections linking learning with a prior experience or related reading				
Understands literal-level concepts				
Uses language to predict and infer				
Understands cause-effect and comparison and can talk about them				
Summarizes main idea from reading				
Produces sentences with noun-verb agreement				
Produces sentences with correct verb tense				
Uses descriptive language to help a listener visualize				
Responds to multiple-meaning words with understanding				

Adapted from Linda Hoyt, Interactive Read-Alouds, © 2007. Portsmouth, NH: Heinemann. Used with permission. May be photocopied for classroom use only.

Reading Levels Tracking Chart also appears on the CD.

Reading Levels Tracking Chart

This *assessment solution* provides a quick overview of progress through levels of reading development—over time. The beauty of this tool is that it allows you to see reading levels at a glance, closely tracking the progress of striving readers in both fiction and nonfiction selections.

To most effectively use this chart, list student names in the left column, then insert dates on which you conferred with a striving reader (during a conference or small-group session) and confirmed that the accuracy rate was above 90% and the student had solid comprehension of a resource at this level using a retell checklist such as the one on page 00 or 00. Please note the key in the Reading Levels Tracking Chart, as it is very important to differentiate between fiction and nonfiction observations to ensure that striving readers are building reading competence in both genre.

Reading Levels Tracking Chart

Key: * = fiction; <u>underline</u> = nonfiction.

Names	Reading Levels																									
	A	B	C	D	E	F	G	H	I	J	K	L	M	N	O	P	Q	R	S	T	U	V	W	X	Y	Z
Alina													9/15* <u>9/22</u>	<u>10/05</u> 10/30*												
Martin			<u>9/7</u>		9/6* <u>9/9</u>		9/10* 9/15* <u>9/17</u>		10/1*		<u>10/5</u> <u>10/8</u>															
Dion								<u>9/6</u> <u>9/8</u>			10/2* 9/14*	<u>10/6</u>														

Reading Levels Tracking Chart

Key: * = fiction; underline = nonfiction. Indicate date when proficiency (90% accuracy and a solid retell) is attained for the level.

Names	Reading Levels																									
	A	B	C	D	E	F	G	H	I	J	K	L	M	N	O	P	Q	R	S	T	U	V	W	X	Y	Z

Comprehension Interview

The Comprehension Interview is an *assessment solution* that helps a close observer guide a striving reader in focusing on and actively using comprehension supports such as determining importance, inferring, summarizing, and so on. With open-ended probes and questions that invite a striving reader to make his thinking transparent, the Comprehension Interview provides support for celebrating progress and planning for comprehension instruction.

As with most assessment tools, it's important to let the learner know what you are doing and what you are hoping to learn about him as a reader. Consider saying, *"Today, I want to learn more about the strategies you are using to help yourself understand a reading selection. I'm going to ask you some questions about your thinking on the selection you read. When I'm finished, I'll share what I learned about you."*

During the interview, jot down evidence of understanding such as quotes from the child's response or your analysis of the response such as in the following example:

Interview Questions for Synthesize/Summarize/Evaluate Provides a summary that captures the main idea and supporting details. Offers evaluative or analytical reflections.	Record Comments or Evidence, Date and Text	Analysis/Next Steps
Can you give me a brief summary of the book?	*Nonfiction:* Frogs Have Sticky Tongues, *4/19. Strong summary with 3 main ideas and supportive details.*	*Recheck in fiction but is progressing nicely in nonfiction.*
If you were to rate this book on a scale of 1–5, what rating would you give it? Why?	*Rating: "I'd give this book a 4 because the author didn't put labels on the diagrams!"*	
What are the strengths and weaknesses of this selection?	*Fiction:* Junie B Jones, *chapter 3, 4/26* *Had difficulty identifying a main idea and offered few supporting details. The lack of picture support may be compromising summative understanding.*	*Provide graphic organizers to focus on big picture understandings. Model think-alouds for main idea and details. Work on visualization to create mental images to support understanding.*

Comprehension Interviews

Reader	Observer Record Comments or Evidence, Date, and Text	Analysis/Next Steps
Visualize Creates mental images of characters, events, and/or ideas. *What did you picture in your mind as you read this part?* *If you were to create an illustration about this, what would you include?*		
Determine Importance Identifies important words and ideas from text. *Which words and ideas do you think are the most important from this text?*		
Connect Makes connections to personal experiences, prior knowledge, or other texts. *Does this selection remind you of anything?* *Can you think of another selection like this one?*		
Question Asks questions to clarify or extend thinking. *What questions did you find yourself asking while you were reading? What did you wonder?* *What questions would you like to ask the author if you had the opportunity?* *What are you wondering now that you have finished this selection?*		

Comprehension Interviews

Reader	Observer Record Comments or Evidence, Date, and Text	Analysis/Next Steps
Infer/Draw Conclusions Reads "between the lines" to capture unstated, but implied, information. Uses information and inferences to draw conclusions about the text. *Why do you think _____ did that?* *In the selection, the subject did ___ and ____. How might you describe that kind of behavior?*		
Synthesize/Summarize/Evaluate Identifies main ideas and supporting details, finds problem and solution in fiction, summarize, integrates information with prior knowledge, offers critical/analytical opinions. *Can you give me a brief summary of the selection?* *How did this selection add to your prior knowledge on ___?* *If you were to rate this book on a scale of 1–5, what rating would you give it? Why?* *What are the strengths and weaknesses of this selection?*		

Use Retells to Scaffold and Assess Understanding

Informal Retell Scoring Guide, Nonfiction Retell Scoring Guide, Fiction Retell Scoring Guide, Retell Self-Reflection: Fiction, and *Retell Self-Reflection: Nonfiction* also appear on the CD.

Retells and Retell Scoring Guides

Retelling is an *assessment solution* that requires striving readers to organize information they have gleaned from a text into a concise summary. Students engaging in retells must review all they know about a text; select key points that reflect main ideas, key events and details, problems, solutions, and setting; then weave the information into a meaningful communication. Retelling has been found to significantly improve comprehension and understanding of story structure while enhancing oral language proficiency (Hoyt 2009b; Allington 2010; de Quiros and Migdalia 2008; Gilliam and Carlile 2007).

Some important understandings about retelling:

- Tell striving readers *why* retelling is important. They need to know how retelling helps them as readers and communicators.

- Do a think-aloud and retell with a focus on an experience you have shared with your striving readers so they can see that you don't tell everything—you select the most important points.

- Self-evaluate your retells in front of striving readers, thinking aloud about the elements you included and your ability to make the retell interesting for a listener.

- Demonstrate retells of fiction selections to model how to focus on problem, solution, characters, and setting.

- Model how to do a nonfiction retell, showing how the retell shifts to a focus on main ideas and supporting details.

- Help striving readers practice retelling short segments of text then progress to longer passages and, finally, entire selections.

- Have students self-reflect on their retells and identify strengths as well as areas for continued practice.

Once striving readers develop an understanding of what is expected in a retell, mentors and coaches can begin to use Retell Scoring Guides to provide quick, formative data collection for monitoring understanding, supporting movement through levels of difficulty in text, and informing next steps in instruction.

Guidelines for Assessing Retells

- Retells and Retell Scoring Guides are designed to be used as a natural part of your one-to-one reading conferences and small-group strategy lessons.

- To launch a retell, provide striving readers with time to reread, reflect, and prepare to share the most important points.

- Cue striving readers with open-ended prompts such as: *Please share the most important things you noticed in this selection. Be sure to tell what this is about and remember that your opinions are welcome too.*

- If a striving reader provides a very limited retell and you suspect that she is capable of more, offer an additional, open-ended prompt such as: *Is there anything you would like to add to your retell? Are there more important ideas that you would like to share? I am really interested in the _____ in this selection. Can you add information about that section?*

- Avoid direct questions such as: Who is the main character? What happened first? Who did _____ in the selection? Those are the questions of a test, not a retell.

- Remember to monitor the authenticity of retelling experiences. If striving readers are asked to retell a reading selection or a life event to an individual who shared the experience or listened to them read the same selection, they may feel that this is a test. To add authenticity, it may help to provide a real audience for the retell whenever possible. Then listen closely and assess as striving readers share a retell with a listener who does not already know all about the book or experience that is the focus of the retell.

- Sometimes, a retell analysis will be done when a student is mid-stream in a reading selection. If that is the case, use your best judgment about what the student understands up to this point in the text. The goal is to support you and your team in gathering quick, informal information that can help you monitor and support movement through levels of text difficulty.

The Retelling Scoring Guides and Self-Reflections that follow offer *assessment* options to guide your thinking and increase the menu of possibility you utilize in gathering rich and varied sources of information on your striving readers.

Informal Retell Scoring Guide

Note to teacher: This Informal Retell support is not for in-depth analysis or benchmarking. It is designed to be used as a natural part of your one-to-one reading conferences and small-group strategy lessons. Sometimes, this analysis will be done when a student is midstream in a reading selection. If that is the case, use your best judgment about what the student understands up to this point in the text. The goal is to support you and your team in gathering quick, informal information that can help you monitor and support movement through levels of text difficulty. Although it is important to record and save the score from this retell in your data collection notebook or on the student's card on the assessment wall, it is not necessary to fill out this form each time you conduct an informal retell. Use it as a guide to analyzing understanding. This level of data collection is designed to support your best intuitive judgment about a student's understanding within *this level of text.*

Prompt for Fiction and Nonfiction Retell:

Tell everything you can about this selection. Be sure to tell what the selection is mostly about and share the ideas that you think are most important.

Nonfiction Retell
(Target Score 10 or Better)

	Points
Main idea statements (2 points each)	
Supporting details (1 point each)	
Use of core academic vocabulary from selection (Maximum 4 points) (Example: When talking about a volcano, the use of magma, chamber, or pressure would be 1 point each if the vocabulary word was in the reading selection and not based on prior knowledge.)	
Evaluative statement about quality of writing, a craft element, text features, or author point of view (2 points)	
A minimum score of 8 needed to move to the next level of text	*Total Score*

Fiction Retell
(Target Score 10 or Better)

	Points
Characters (1 point)	
Setting (1 point)	
Problem (1 point)	
Solution (1 point)	
Main idea statement (1 point)	
Significant events in order (3 points) (Can earn 1 of 3 or 2 of 3 if events are incomplete or out of order.)	
Evaluative statement about quality of writing, craft element, story attribute, or character (2 points)	
A minimum score of 8 needed to move to the next level of text	*Total Score*

L. Hoyt, K. Davis, J. Olson, and K. Boswell, Solutions for Reading Comprehension, © 2011. Portsmouth, NH: Heinemann. May be photocopied for classroom use only.

Nonfiction Retell Scoring Guide

Reader:	Date:
Title of selection used for retell:	Level:
Observer/recorder:	

	Observations and Next Steps
6 The reader states more than one main idea and provides supporting details for each. Key concepts are understood and presented accurately. Subject-specific vocabulary is woven naturally into the retell. The reader looks a listener in the eye during much of the retell. The reader refers to or shows key points in the text or a visual. The text is referenced in the retell. On page _____, it stated that _____. There is a well-supported, evaluative statement or personal response about the text that may include a focus on a conclusion, quality of writing, visuals, ongoing questions, inferences, a craft element, use of text features, coverage of the topic, and so on.	
4 The reader is able to state one main idea and provide supporting details. Most concepts are understood and presented accurately in the retell. A few subject-specific words are included. The reader provides some eye contact with the listener. The reader may refer to the text or a visual. There is a well-supported personal response to the text. Beyond the text extensions such as conclusion, inferences, ongoing questions may be present.	
2 The reader provides details but no main ideas. A small number of concepts are understood and presented in the retell. Some inaccuracies or shallow understandings may be evident. A minimal number of subject-specific words are included. There is little eye contact with a listener. The reader is clearly dependent on the book during the recount. No opinions are offered. There is no reference to the text or text features.	

Adapted from Linda Hoyt, Revisit, Reflect Retell, *Updated Edition, © 2009. Portsmouth, NH: Heinemann. Used with permission. May be photocopied for classroom use only.*

Fiction Retell Scoring Guide

	Observations and Next Steps
Reader:	Date:
Title of selection used for retell:	Level:
Observer/recorder:	

	Observations and Next Steps
6 **Characters** Describes all main and supporting characters Describes traits of main characters **Plot** Provides analysis, including inferences Makes personal connections to the story Retells main and secondary events in order with detail **Theme** Relates a message that demonstrates understanding of sociocultural or human issues **Setting** Includes specific details about place or time **Problem–Solution** Describes problem and resolution Designates climax May evaluate tension level **Response** Well-supported personal response	
4 **Characters** Identifies all main characters Describes some character traits **Plot** Includes a description of key events in order; includes main idea, beginning, middle, and end **Setting** Accurate information about time and place **Problem–Solution** Can identify problem and resolution **Response** Well-supported personal response	
2 **Characters** Names some characters **Plot** Vague idea of the topic or character development Limited summary Limited understanding of author's message **Problem–Solution** Limited or missing **Response** Not present	

Adapted from Linda Hoyt, Revisit, Reflect Retell, Updated Edition, © 2009. Portsmouth, NH: Heinemann. Used with permission. May be photocopied for classroom use only.

Retell Self-Reflection: Fiction

Reader _____ Story _____ Date _____

In my retell I remembered to: (✓)

_____ Look at the audience and make eye contact

_____ Think about the story

_____ Speak clearly and loudly enough for all to hear

_____ Tell the most important parts and why they are important

I included:

_____ The beginning

_____ The middle

_____ The end

_____ The problem

_____ The solution

_____ Interesting details about the characters

_____ Facts about the setting

My opinion about the selection: Why I think it is or is not a good story.

Rating my retell:

My rating of my retell today: _____ (1–5). I deserve this rating because

_____. I am getting better at _____. I still need to work a

little harder on _____.

L. Hoyt, K. Davis, J. Olson, and K. Boswell, Solutions for Reading Comprehension, © 2011. Portsmouth, NH: Heinemann. May be photocopied for classroom use only.

Retell Self-Reflection: Nonfiction

Reader _____ Story _____ Date _____

I prepared for the retell by: (✓)

____ Rereading the selection

____ Listing or drawing main ideas that my audience should hear

____ Selecting an important picture or diagram that my audience should see

____ Practicing the retell in my head or into a tape recorder

During the retell, I remembered to:

____ Make eye contact

____ Speak clearly

____ Include main ideas about my topic

____ Show an important picture or diagram

____ Use key words from my reading to teach about the topic

____ Offer an opinion or an evaluation about the selection, the writing, the visuals, or the author's work

Rating my retell:

On a scale of 1–5, I think this retell deserves a _____ because_____.

I am particularly proud that I remembered to _____. Next time,

I will also remember to _____.

Reader Response: Written Reflections

Reader Response: Written Reflections is a thinking scaffold and *assessment solution* that offers teachers a helpful view of the insights and understandings held by a striving reader. In a reader response log, striving readers respond to the texts they are reading by recording predictions, reactions, questions, and summaries. There is substantial evidence to support the importance of having learners write in response to their reading as a way to reprocess and reflect upon the content (Pearson 2008; Cloud, Genese, and Hamayan 2009; Dragan 2005; Howard 2010; Klingner, Vaughn, and Boardman 2007).

As in all situations where we want striving readers to produce the best possible work, it is important to model how you respond to your own reading through writing. After reading a passage, you could think aloud about your response to a selection and then *show* your striving readers how you could turn your thinking into a reader response reflection. Once your striving readers understand what you want them to do, they can work with you to create an anchor chart listing options for entries in a response journal—making sure to include response options for both fiction and nonfiction.

Striving readers love to meet with partners to share the reader response entries and have conversations about the resources they are reading. This gives them an authentic audience and a clear sense of purpose for the responses they are writing.

From an assessment view, teachers can then collect the reader responses and analyze them for depth of understanding, writing proficiencies, accuracy of information, and so on.

Writing Stems for Reader Response Entries

- I wonder . . .

- I was surprised when . . .

- This reminds me of . . .

- When _____ happened, it made me think of _____.

- I learned . . .

- I noticed . . .

- I liked . . .

- I had trouble understanding . . .

- I felt _____ when I read about _____.

- One striking image from the book is _____.

- If I could talk to _____ (character from the book), I would say

  _____.

- I wonder why the author _____.

Teach Students to
Read Different
Kinds of Text—
Differently

Reflecting on Pace: A Self-Reflection
appears full size on the CD.

Assess and Coach for Effective Pacing

Oral reading with pacing that is differentiated according to the kind of text being read is important for striving readers. First, striving readers must learn to read different kinds of texts—differently. A recipe or set of directions needs to be read in small chunks so readers can perform a needed action, then read a bit more—and engage in another action. A standardized test requires that striving readers first read a passage, then quickly move back and forth between a series of questions, scanning the passage to confirm answer choices. On the other hand, a lively Shel Silverstein poem or a tension-filled paragraph in *Hatchet* calls for "full speed ahead" reading to completely experience the best that those selections have to offer.

In addition, striving readers need to understand that pacing needs to be adjusted according to a reader's purpose. If the purpose for reading is to savor the nuances of the menu in a fine-dining restaurant, it is natural to slow down and engage in a lot of rereading. If the purpose is to figure out which beverage to order at a fast-food establishment, a reader only needs a fast scan to make sure their beverage of choice is listed. If the purpose is to digest a math story problem, savor a somber poem, or concentrate on the digestive system of a reptile, readers need to take things slowly.

As striving readers develop an understanding of how pace, purpose, and text difficulty affect their behavior as a reader, coaches and mentors can support their continued growth by assessing the choices striving readers are making about pacing and coaching them to higher levels of sophistication in this important understanding.

With these pacing differences in mind, it is important that striving readers not be subjected to timed readings that present a message that faster is always better. To survive the increasingly complex resources they will read in school, striving readers must learn to analyze their purpose for reading, the complexity of the reading material, and the accessibility of the text; then consciously decide which rate will best help them understand the content and achieve their purpose for reading. This metacognitive stance to pacing helps striving readers develop a conscious and thoughtful approach to different texts that will improve comprehension and increase their flexibility as a reader.

Reflecting on Pace: A Self-Reflection

Reader _____

Text Read	Purpose for Reading	Difficulty Level (Easy, Medium, Difficult)	Importance of Task	My Pace Will Be _____	After Reading Reflection: How effective was the pacing? Would you pace the reading differently next time?
Math: geometry story problems	Solve the problem	Difficult	Very! (I need to get this right.)	Slow	Rereading
Announcement about carnival	Awareness of date and time	Easy	Not too important	Fast	Skim the headings; notice date and time.
Poetry by Greenfield	Understand and write a response	Medium	Important	Slow	Reread, visualize, connect

Reflecting on Pace: A Self-Reflection

Reader _____

Text Read	Purpose for Reading	Difficulty Level (Easy, Medium, Difficult)	Importance of Task	My Pace Will Be _____	After Reading Reflection: How effective was the pacing? Would you pace the reading differently next time?

Oral Reading Scoring Guides

Expressive oral reading helps striving readers sound like great readers. When they produce oral reading that is fluent, confident, and supported by expressive intonation and pacing, they feel terrific about themselves and the act of being a reader. In addition, evidence suggests that when readers are expressive, responding to punctuation, phrasing, and intonation, they experience elevated levels of comprehension (Pressley, Gaskins, and Fingeret 2006; Chard, Vaughn, and Tyler 2002; Rasinski 2003; Allington 2010).

To help you assess and support expressive oral reading, the following rubrics and scoring guides offer a range of possibilities and orientations toward expressive and fluent oral production.

Because striving readers tend to have poor self-images about themselves as readers, it is best to save oral reading for times when you and a vulnerable reader are together in the privacy of a reading conference or introduce it when a striving reader has rehearsed a reading passage and is prepared to perform it with drama and expression. It is especially important to avoid round-robin reading with striving readers as having an audience adds a significant level of stress for the learner, and there is little benefit from having tangled readers listen to other tangled readers read out loud (Opitz and Rasinski 2009).

As you use the following scoring guides, please be sure to note that there is a separate score generated for each dimension of expressive oral reading. These separated scores are important for striving readers as it allows coaches and mentors, as well as striving readers themselves, to target specific behaviors that will most contribute to improving their expressive oral reading.

Expressive Oral Reading Scoring Guide I

Reader_____ Date_____

	1	2	3	4	
Phrasing	Reads word by word, hesitates often, rarely rereads	Reads in short (two- to three-word) phrases, little attention to punctuation	Reads in longer-meaning phrases most of the time	Consistently reads in longer phrases, sounds fluent and like conversation	Phrasing score _____
Rate	Rate is slow with long pauses, sounds words out	May be too slow or too fast, does not reflect understanding of message in text	Mostly smooth and at a rate that is appropriate for the text	Rate varies in response to text demands, indicates attention to message	Rate score _____
Expression	Reading does not sound natural or conversational, monotone	Reading sounds conversational some of the time, especially dialogue	Reading sounds conversational most of the time, voice rises and falls appropriately	Reading consistently sounds like conversation	Expression score _____
Punctuation	Ignores punctuation	Inconsistent attention to punctuation	Some attention to punctuation	Consistently attends to punctuation	Punctuation score _____

Instructional Plan for Expressive Oral Reading:

Area of instruction (phrasing, rate, expression, punctuation) to target with modeling and coaching:

_____

Instructional steps to lift learner performance: _____

The classroom teacher will _____. The specialist(s) will

_____.

Expressive Oral Reading Scoring Guide II

Reader_____ Date_____

Criteria	4	3	2	1	
Adjustment of reading rate	Reader adjusts reading rate based on the kind of text and the purpose for reading.	The reader speeds up or slows down even when the reading does not warrant it.	The reader fails to adjust rate based on the genre and purpose for reading.	The reader reads either too slowly or too quickly.	Rate score _____
Attention to punctuation	Reader attends to punctuation and adjusts voice accordingly.	The reader may demonstrate a few errors in punctuation but they do not affect meaning or phrasing.	Punctuation is occasionally ignored and phrasing is affected. As a result, the meaning begins to be distorted.	Reader frequently ignores punctuation. Meaning is distorted.	Punctuation score _____
Expression	Intonation and emotions match the author's purpose.	Reader shows limited emotion, but the author's meaning is still intact.	The reader lacks intonation and emotion, interfering with meaning.	Very little intonation or emotion. The student reads in a monotone.	Expression score _____
Pacing	Reading is well paced, smooth, and expressive. Pauses are deliberate, for effect.	Reading is well paced. Occasional slowing may be present when student encounters difficulty.	Reading is either too slow or too fast.	Reading is halting, disfluent, and slow.	Pacing score _____

L. Hoyt, K. Davis, J. Olson, and K. Boswell, Solutions for Reading Comprehension, *© 2011. Portsmouth, NH: Heinemann. May be photocopied for classroom use only.*

Reader_____ Observer_____

For each observation, identify the rating for pacing, intonation, punctuation, and confidence. Select only one rating for each category in each observation.

Possible Points	Pacing	Observation 1	Observation 2	Observation 3	Observation 4	Observation 5	Observation 6
4	Pacing is smooth and flows well, matching the text and the purpose for reading.						
3	Reading flows well except for occasional challenges with the text.						
2	Pacing is too slow or too fast for text and purpose.						
1	Pacing is slow and word by word.						
Possible Points	Intonation	Observation 1	Observation 2	Observation 3	Observation 4	Observation 5	Observation 6
4	Intonation and expression reflect the meaning and style of the text.						
3	Intonation is meaningful but occasionally includes exaggerations or inflections inappropriate to the text.						
2	Intonation lacks enthusiasm overall but occasionally words are joined into meaningful phrases.						
1	Intonation is flat with little interpretation of text.						

Implications for instruction:

Reader_____ Observer_____

For each observation, identify the rating for pacing, intonation, punctuation, and confidence. Select only one rating for each category in each observation.

Possible Points	Punctuation	Observation 1	Observation 2	Observation 3	Observation 4	Observation 5	Observation 6
4	Reader demonstrates effective use of punctuation to support phrasing and intonation.						
3	Reader sometimes uses punctuation to support phrasing.						
2	Punctuation is used ineffectively. Sometimes it is ignored. Other times pauses are too long or too short in response to the punctuation.						
1	Reader frequently ignores punctuation causing phrasing and flow of reading to be confusing.						
Possible Points	Confidence	Observation 1	Observation 2	Observation 3	Observation 4	Observation 5	Observation 6
4	Reading is fluent, confident, and accurate. Reader appears comfortable and in control.						
3	Reading is mostly fluent and confident. The reader occasionally hesitates and appears to lose confidence.						
2	Reader lacks confidence much of the time. There are pauses and moments of word-by-word reading. May look at the teacher as plea for assistance.						
1	Reader demonstrates word-by-word reading with minimal confidence and little fluency.						

Implications for instruction:

Student Observation Record: Word-Solving Strategies

Striving readers need to have a broad range of word-solving strategies in hand when they approach challenging texts. With a wide array of word-solving moves that go beyond "sound it out," striving readers are empowered to use all available cues and can more easily navigate sight words and nondecodable challenges.

A Student Observation Record is an *assessment solution* that allows teachers to determine what word-solving strategies striving readers are using consistently.

To complete the observation record, simply record the date and the title of the text that is being read by the child. Then, listen as the child reads. Pay close attention to what the reader does when encountering a new word. Place a check mark next to the strategies that you observe the student using each time you observe. The benefit to this form is its ability to monitor word-solving strategy use across multiple texts, demonstrating which behaviors a striving reader has fully internalized and can carry across multiple texts.

Once you have completed the observation record sheet, you can begin to analyze it for patterns of reading behavior. During your analysis of progress, you may want to wonder: Does the student rely almost exclusively on initial sounds when he encounters a new word? Does he look for chunks of the word that he knows? When he solves the word, does he reread to regain meaning or fluency?

Once you have observed the student over time, you can determine what strategies you can teach the student as you move forward.

Student Observation Record: Word-Solving Strategies

Student_____ Observer_____

Observation #1   Date _____   Text _____

Observation #2   Date _____   Text _____

Observation #3   Date _____   Text _____

Observation #4   Date _____   Text _____

Observation #5   Date _____   Text _____

Place a ✓ next to any of the following word-solving strategies that the reader demonstrated.

	#1	#2	#3	#4	#5	#6
Checks the picture for clues						
Uses context clues						
Rereads for fluency						
Rereads to regain meaning						
Checks medial sounds						
Uses ending sounds						
Uses initial sounds						
Reads on to determine meanings of unknown words						
Chunks words						
Onset/rime						
Syllables						
Familiar parts						

Assess Skills in Word Construction

Striving readers can and should have experiences in constructing words as well as decoding or deconstructing them. In this *assessment solution*, striving readers can work with letter tiles or small squares of paper with one letter per square to construct words related to a familiar topic or a book that has been previously read. It is important to work with words related to a familiar topic or book so that striving readers always remember that reading must make sense. One of the greatest tools readers bring to reading is an innate orientation to make sense. With a focus on word parts within the context of a meaningful unit of study, striving readers have the advantage of high-quality word study in concert with content area vocabulary.

Striving readers in the middle grades can also deconstruct words, taking content-specific words and cutting them apart to show syllables, base words, endings, and so on.

The goal is to have striving readers work with high-impact vocabulary at the same time they examine the internal workings of each word. As words are constructed, the close observer can note which students are comfortable building words and which striving readers have strong control over consonants, vowels, word beginnings and endings, or syllable identification. The opportunity for both instruction and assessment within a word construction experience is rich and varied.

The kinesthetic nature of word construction is highly engaging for striving readers and helps them focus on word parts.

An example for primary grades: After reading a selection about the life cycle of a frog, striving readers might work with letter tiles to construct words such as: *egg* (three-letter word), *frog* (four-letter word), *hatch* (five-letter word), *hatched* (add an ending to change the base word), *caterpillar* (multisyllable word), and so on.

An example for middle grades: At the middle grades, a word construction experience might focus on westward migration and include words such as: *log* (three-letter word), *cabin* (five-letter word), *settlement* (multisyllable word), *migrate* and *migration* (add an ending to change the base word).

Over time, word construction experiences can offer assessment opportunities for any imaginable word pattern, phonic understanding, or morphological structure.

Assessing Word Construction Skills

Student_____ Observer_____

Use vocabulary from a current unit of study, familiar topic, or familiar book to engage striving readers in constructing words. Observe closely as readers build words and focus on word parts.

	Observation #1 Date: _____ Today we constructed words related to: _____ _____ (topic)	**Observation #2** Date: _____ Today we constructed words related to: _____ _____ (topic)	**Observation #3** Date: _____ Today we constructed words related to: _____ _____ (topic)
	Note which words were created and whether the student constructed the word independently.		
Create words with three letters			
Create words with four letters			
Create words with five or more letters			
Change the beginning or ending sound to create a new word			
Create a word with more than one syllable			
Add an ending to change the base word			
Identify the number of syllables in a word			
Relate the meaning of a word that has been "chunked" to the passage and explain its importance			

Adapted from Linda Hoyt, Make It Real, © 2002. Portsmouth, NH: Heinemann. Used with permission. May be photocopied for classroom use only.

Phonic Writing Analysis

When students are asked to identify a letter and name its sound on a card, that striving reader is operating at a level of simple recognition. There is no indication from that level of assessment that a striving reader can use the target sound in reading or in writing. On the other hand, if writing samples are gathered and analyzed to see which letters, sounds, word parts, and grammatical elements are used, the phonic understandings are being measured at the application level. Here are data—real evidence that a striving reader not only recognizes a letter, sound, or word part, she is able to use it in an authentic writing task. This *assessment solution* is one of the most powerful phonic assessments you could possibly use as it measures letter knowledge at the point of use, writing.

To use a phonic writing analysis, simply gather several unedited writing samples from a striving learner and, using the following chart, tally each time a sound–symbol relationship is utilized. It is important to use tally marks when a letter, a sound, or a word part has been used. Then, over time and several pieces of writing, you will be able to collect evidence that the understanding has been used multiple times and resides in long-term memory.

This tool will help you be highly diagnostic in identifying learner strengths as well as phonic understandings that need supportive instruction. With a Phonic Writing Analysis, you can focus your instruction on the letters and sounds that are emerging as evidenced by a small number of tally marks. For sound–symbol relationships for which you find no evidence in writing, instruction will need to begin with an introduction to the letter or phoneme to move the striving reader to a higher level of awareness with that particular phonetic understanding.

Careful use of the Phonic Writing Analysis increases instructional value because you can target supports directly to student needs and not waste valuable time on letters and sounds that students already know.

Best of all, the Phonic Writing Analysis makes it easy to identify a group of learners who share a need for support with a particular phonetic element. A quick look at the chart will help you identify students who would benefit from a small-group minilesson focused on a sound that they need to bring into their repertoire of sound–symbol relationships.

(✓) student analysis
( ) demonstration checklist

	NAME	b	c	d	f	g	h	j	k	l	m	n	p	q	r	s	t	x	w	x	y	z	a	e	i	o	u	sh	ch	th	wh	Silent e
2	Andre																															
3	Juanelle																															
4	Malo																															
5	Jordan																															
6	Alara																															
7	Dasia																															
8	Justin																															
9	Erica																															
10	Teriro																															
11	Hasib																															

Phonic Writing Analysis

( ) student analysis
( ) demonstration checklist

Names	b	c	d	f	g	h	j	k	l	m	n	p	q	r	s	t	v	w	x	y	z	a	e	i	o	u	sh	ch	th	wh	Silent
1																															
2																															
3																															
4																															
5																															
6																															
7																															
8																															
9																															
10																															
11																															
12																															
13																															
14																															
15																															
16																															
17																															
18																															
19																															

From Linda Hoyt, Snapshots, © 2000. Portsmouth, NH: Heinemann. Used with permission. May be photocopied for classroom use only.

Coauthors (from left to right) Kelly Davis, Jane Olson, Linda Hoyt, and Kelly Boswell with their editor, Harvey "Smokey" Daniels.

Nationally recognized literacy consultant **Linda Hoyt** creates environments where engaged children are active participants in their own learning. She is the author or editor of *Revisit, Reflect, Retell*, Updated Edition; *Spotlight on Comprehension*; *Exploring Informational Texts*; *Make It Real*; and *Snapshots* as well as *Snapshots* the DVD and the *Navigating Informational Texts* staff development DVD; and the author of the *first*hand *Interactive Read-Alouds* series and the co-author of the *first*hand *Explorations in Nonfiction Writing* series with Tony Stead—all published by Heinemann.

Kelly Davis has thirty years of experience as a general education and special education teacher. She currently serves as a Department of Special Education Resource Teacher for the Howard County Public School System in Ellicott City, Maryland and does consulting.

Jane Beecher Olson is a literacy trainer for special education teachers. She has been a classroom, special education, and Reading Recovery teacher and also does consulting.

Kelly Boswell's combined love for children and literacy has fueled a passion to become a lifelong learner and advocate for striving learners. She has taught first, second, and fourth grade during her eighteen years in education; served as a District Literacy Specialist and K–2 Literacy Coach; and currently works as an educational consultant.

Alexander, K., D. Entwisle, and L. Olson. 2007. "Lasting Consequences of the Summer Learning Gap." *American Sociological Review* 72 (2): 167–180.

Allington, R. L. 1980. "Poor Readers Don't Get to Read Much in Reading Groups." *Language Arts* 57 (8): 872–77.

———. 2002. "You Can't Learn Much from Books You Can't Read." *Educational Leadership* 60 (3): 16–19.

———. 2006. *What Really Matters for Struggling Readers.* Boston, MA: Pearson.

———. 2009. *What Really Matters in Fluency, Research-Based Practices Across the Curriculum.* Boston, MA: Pearson Education.

———. 2010. *Essential Readings on Struggling Learners.* Newark, DE: International Reading Association.

Applegate, M., K. Quinn, and A. Applegate. 2008. *The Critical Reading Inventory: Assessing Students: Reading and Thinking.* Upper Saddle River, NJ: Pearson.

Au, K. H. 2010. "Culturally Responsive Instruction." *Reading Today* 27 (3): 30–31.

Baker, L., M. Dreher, and J. Guthrie, eds. 2000. *Engaging Young Readers.* New York: Guilford.

Barrentine, S., and S. Stokes. 2005. *Reading Assessment: Principles and Practices for Elementary Teachers.* Newark, DE: International Reading Association.

Baumann, J. F., and E. J. Kame'enui. 2004. *Vocabulary Instruction.* New York: Guilford.

Beck, I. L., M. G. McKeown, and L. Kucan. 2002. *Bringing Words to Life.* New York: Guilford.

Beers, K. 2001. *Reading Strategies Handbook.* Austin, TX: Holt, Reinhart & Winston.

———. 2003. *When Kids Can't Read: What Teachers Can Do.* Portsmouth, NH: Heinemann.

Bender, W. 2002. *Differentiating Instruction for Students with Learning Disabilities: Best Teaching Practices for General and Special Educators.* Thousand Oaks, CA: Corwin.

Borman, G., K. Wong, L. Hedges, and J. D'Agostino. 2003. "Coordinating Categorical and Regular Programs: Effects on Title I Students' Educational Opportunities and Outcomes." In *Title I: Compensatory Education at the Crossroads*, edited by G. D. Borman, S. D. Stringfield, and R. E. Slavin, pp. 79–116. Mahwah, NJ: Erlbaum.

Boushey, G., and J. Moser. 2006. *The Daily 5.* Portland, ME: Stenhouse.

———. 2009. *The Café Book.* Portland, ME: Stenhouse.

Britton, J. 1992. *Language and Learning: The Importance of Speech in Children's Development.* Portsmouth, NH: Boynton/Cook.

Brozo, W. 2010. "The Role of Content Literacy in an Effective RTI Program." *The Reading Teacher* 64 (2):147–50.

Brozo, W., and M. Simpson. 2007. *Content Literacy for Today's Adolescents: Honoring Diversity and Building Competence.* Upper Saddle River, NJ: Merrill Prentice Hall.

Calkins, L. M., K. Montgomery, and D. Santman. 1998. *A Teacher's Guide to Standardized Reading Tests: Knowledge Is Power.* Portsmouth, NH: Heinemann.

Cary, S. 2007. *Working with English Language Learners: Answers to Teachers Top Ten Questions.* Portsmouth, NH: Heinemann.

Caswell, L. J., and N. K. Duke. 1998. "Non-narratives as a Catalyst for Literacy Development." *Language Arts* 78: 108–17.

Chard, D. J., S. Vaughn, and B. J. Tyler, 2002. "A Synthesis of Research on Effective Interventions for Building Reading Fluency with Elementary Students with Learning Disabilities." *Journal of Learning Disabilities* 35 (5): 386–406.

Clay, M. M. 2002. *An Observation Survey of Early Literacy Achievement.* Portsmouth, NH: Heinemann.

———. 2005. *Literacy Lessons Designed for Individuals, Part Two, Teaching Procedures.* Portsmouth, NH: Heinemann.

Cloud, N., F. Genese, and E. Hamayan. 2009. *Literacy Instruction for English Language Learners.* Portsmouth, NH: Heinemann.

Coffey, H. 2009. *Formative Assessment.* Chapel Hill, NC: University of North Carolina LearnNC.

Cohen, D., and S. Moffit. 2009. *The Ordeal of Equality: Did Federal Regulation Fix the Schools?* Cambridge, MA: Harvard University Press.

Common Core State Standards. 2010. Washington, DC: Council of Chief State School Officers and the National Governors Association.

Cooper, J. D., D. J. Chard, and N. D. Kieger. 2006. *The Struggling Reader: Interventions That Work.* New York: Scholastic.

Cummins, J. 2009. "Literacy and English-Language Learners: A Shifting Landscape for Students, Teachers, Researchers, and Policy Makers." *Educational Researcher* 38 (5): 382–84.

Cunningham, P. M. 1995. *Phonics They Use, Words for Reading and Writing.* New York: HarperCollins College Publishers.

———. 2003. In *Best Practices in Literacy Instruction*, 2d ed., edited by L. M. Morrow, L. B. Gambrell, and M. Pressley. New York: Guilford Press.

Cunningham, P. M., and R. L. Allington. 1999. *Classrooms That Work: They Can All Read and Write.* New York: Addison Wesley Longman.

Cunningham, P. M., and J. W. Cunningham. 2002. "What We Know About How to Teach Phonics." In *What Research Has to Say About Reading Instruction*, edited by A. Farstrup and J. Samuels. Newark, DE: International Reading Association.

Daniels, H., A. Hyde, and S. Zemelman. (Forthcoming.) *Best Practice, Fourth Edition: Today's Standards for Teaching and Learning in America's Schools.* Portsmouth, NH: Heinemann.

de Quiros, C., and A. Migdalia. 2008. *Structured Story Reading and Retell Related to Listening Comprehension and Vocabulary Acquisition Among English Language Learners.* Austin, TX: Texas A and M.

Denton, D., S. Vaughn, and J. Fletcher. 2003. "Bringing Research-Based Practice in Reading Intervention to Scale." *Learning Disabilities Research and Practice* 18 (3): 201–11.

Dorn, L., and C. Soffos. 2005. *Teaching for Deep Comprehension: A Reading Workshop Approach.* Portland, ME: Stenhouse.

Dragan, P. 2005. *A How-to Guide for Teaching English Language Learners.* Portsmouth, NH: Heinemann.

Dreher, M., and J. Gray 2009. "Compare, Contrast, Comprehend: Using Compare-Contrast Structures with ELLs in K–3 Classrooms." *The Reading Teacher* 63 (2): 132–41.

Duke, N. 2000. "3–6 Minutes Per Day: The Scarcity of Informational Text in First Grade." *Reading Research Quarterly* 35 (2): 202–24.

Duke, N., and P. D. Pearson. 2002. "Effective Practices for Developing Reading Comprehension." In *What Research Has to Say About Reading Instruction*, 3d ed., edited by A. Farstrup and J. Samuels. Newark, DE: International Reading Association.

Duke, N., and V. Bennett-Armistead. 2003. *Reading and Writing Informational Text in the Primary Grades.* New York: Scholastic.

Echevarria, J., M. E. Vogt, and D. Short. 2008. *Making Content Comprehensible for English Learners: The SIOP® Model.* Boston, MA: Allyn and Bacon.

Fisher, D., and N. Frey. 2001. "Access to the Core Curriculum: Critical Ingredients for Success." *Remedial and Special Education* 22 (3): 148–57.

———. 2008. *Better Learning Through Structured Teaching.* Alexandria, VA: ASCD.

Fountas, I., and G. S. Pinnell. 1996. *Guided Reading: Good First Teaching for All Children.* Portsmouth, NH: Heinemann.

———. 2006. *Teaching for Comprehending and Fluency.* Portsmouth, NH: Heinemann.

Freeman, Y. S., and D. E. Freeman. 2004. "Connecting Students to Culturally Relevant Texts." *Talking Points* 15 (2).

———. 2009. *Academic Language for English Language Learners and Struggling Readers, How to Help Students Succeed Across the Content Areas.* Portsmouth, NH: Heinemann.

Fuchs, D., L. Fuchs, and S. Vaughn, eds. 2008. *Response to Intervention: A Framework for Reading Educators.* Newark, DE: International Reading Association. Co-published with Corwin Press.

Gay, G. 2000. *Culturally Responsive Teaching: Theory, Research, & Practice.* New York: Teachers College Press.

Gersten, R., D. Compton, D. Connor, J. Dimino, L. Santoro, and S. Linan-Thompson. 2008. *Assisting Students Struggling with Reading: Response to Intervention and Multi-Tier Intervention for Reading in the Primary Grades* (NCEE 2009-4045). Washington, DC: National Center for Education Evaluation and Regional Assistance, Institute of Education Sciences, U.S. Department of Education. Available at: http://ies.ed.gov/ncee/wwc/publications/practiceguides. Accessed April 24, 2010.

Gill, Chamkaur. 2008. "Motivating English-Language Learners Through Drama Techniques." *The Journal of INTI International Education Group* (Special issue on teaching and learning): 43–51.

Gilliam, R., and R. Carlile. 2007. "Oral Reading and Story Retelling of Students with Specific Language Impairment." *Language, Speech, and Hearing Services in Schools* 28.

Goodman, K. 1969. "Analysis of Oral Reading Miscues: Applied Psycholinguistics." In *Language and Literacy: The Selected Writings of Kenneth Goodman*, Vol. I, edited by F. Gollasch, pp. 123–34. Boston: Routledge & Kegan Paul.

Goodman, Y., D. Watson, and C. Burke. 2005. *Reading Miscue Inventory.* Katonah, NY: Richard C. Owen.

Goswami, U. 2000. "Phonological and Lexical Processes." In *Handbook of Reading Research*, Vol. 3, edited by M. L. Kamil, P. B. Mosenthal, P. D. Pearson, and R. Barr, pp. 251–67. Mahwah, NH: Erlbaum.

Graves, D. 1999. *Bring Life into Learning.* Portsmouth, NH: Heinemann.

Graves, M. F. 2006. *The Vocabulary Book*. New York: Teachers College Press.

Griffith, L. W., and T. V. Rasinski. 2004. "A Focus on Fluency: How One Teacher Incorporated Fluency in Her Reading Curriculum." *Reading Teacher* 58: 126–37.

Guthrie, J. T., and N. M. Humenick. 2004. "Motivating Students to Read: Evidence for Classroom Practices That Increase Motivation and Achievement." In *The Voice of Evidence in Reading Research*, edited by P. D. McCardle and V. Chhabra, pp. 329–54. Baltimore: Brookes.

Hall, D. P., and P. M. Cunningham. 2009. *Making Words: Grade K: 50 Interactive Lessons That Build Phonemic Awareness, Phonics, and Spelling Skills*. Boston: Pearson.

Hamman, P., and T. Rasinski. 2010. "Fluency: Why It Is Not Hot." *Reading Today* 28.

Harvey, S., and A. Goudvis. 2007. *Strategies That Work, Teaching Comprehension for Understanding and Engagement*. Portland, ME: Stenhouse.

Harvey, S., and H. Daniels. 2009. *Collaboration and Comprehension: Inquiry Circles in Action*. Portsmouth, NH: Heinemann.

Harwayne, S. 1999. *Going Public*. Portsmouth, NH: Heinemann.

Hayes, D., and J. Grether. 1983. "The School Year and Vacations: When Do Students Learn?" *The Cornell Journal of Social Relations* 17 (1): 56–71.

Hiebert, E. H., P. D. Pearson, B. M. Taylor, V. Richardson, and S. G. Paris. 1998. *Every Child a Reader: Applying Research in the Classroom*. Ann Arbor, MI: CIERA/University of Michigan.

Howard, Mary 2010. *Moving Forward with RTI: Reading and Writing Activities for Every Instructional Setting and Tier*. Portsmouth, NH: Heinemann.

Hoyt, L. 2000. *Snapshots: Literacy Minilessons Up Close*. Portsmouth, NH: Heinemann.

———. 2002. *Make It Real: Strategies for Success with Informational Text*. Portsmouth, NH: Heinemann.

———. 2005. *Spotlight on Comprehension: Building a Literacy of Thoughtfulness*. Portsmouth, NH: Heinemann.

———. 2007. *Interactive Read-Alouds*. Portsmouth, NH: Heinemann.

———. 2009a. "Interactive Literacy: Reading, Thinking, Taking a More Active Stance." The Summer Literacy Institute, Presentation at Hamline University, St. Paul, MN.

———. 2009b. *Revisit, Reflect, Retell, Updated Edition*. Portsmouth, NH: Heinemann.

Hoyt, L., M. Mooney, and B. Parkes. 2003. *Exploring Informational Texts: From Theory to Practice*. Portsmouth, NH: Heinemann.

Hoyt, L., and T. Therriault. 2008. *Mastering the Mechanics: Ready-to-Use Lessons for Modeled, Guided, and Independent Editing*. New York: Scholastic.

Jenkins, S. 2009. "How to Maintain School Reading Success: Five Recommendations from a Struggling Male Reader." *The Reading Teacher* 963 (2): 159–62.

Jensen, E. 2005. *Teaching with the Brain in Mind*. Alexandria, VA: ASCD.

Jeong, J., J. Gaffney, and J. Choi. 2010. "Availability and Use of Informational Texts in Second-, Third-, and Fourth-Grade Classrooms." *Research in the Teaching of English* 44 (4): 435–56.

Johnson, P. 2006. *One Child at a Time: Making the Most of Your Time with Struggling Readers*. Portsmouth, NH: Heinemann.

Johnson, P., and K. Keier. 2010. *Catching Readers Before They Fall*. Portland, ME: Stenhouse.

Keene, E. O., et al. 2011. *Comprehension Moving Forward*. Portsmouth, NH: Heinemann.

Keene, E. O., and S. Zimmerman. 2007. *Mosaic of Thought: The Power of Comprehension Strategy Instruction*, 2d ed. Portsmouth, NH: Heinemann.

Kendall, J., and O. Khoun. 2005. *Making Sense: Small-Group Comprehension Lessons for English Language Learners*. Portland, ME: Stenhouse.

Kintsch, W., and E. Kintsch. 2005. "Comprehension." In *Current Issues on Reading Comprehension and Assessment*, edited by S. G. Paris and S. A. Stahl, pp. 71092. Mahwah, NJ: Erlbaum.

Kletzien, S. 2009. "Paraphrasing: An Effective Comprehension Strategy." *The Reading Teacher* 636 (1): 73–77.

Klingner, J. K., S. Vaughn, and A. Boardman 2007. *Teaching Reading Comprehension to Students with Learning Difficulties*. New York: Guilford Press.

Kluth, P. 2003. *You're Going to Love This Kid: Teaching Students with Autism in the Inclusive Classroom*. Baltimore: Paul H. Brooks.

———. 2007. *A Land We Can Share: Teaching Literacy to Students with Autism*. Baltimore: Paul H. Brooks.

Krashen, S. 2003. *Explorations in Language Acquisition and Use*. Portsmouth, NH: Heinemann.

———. 2004. *The Power of Reading: Insights from Research*. Portsmouth, NH: Heinemann.

Li, D., and S. Nes. 2001. "Using Paired Reading to Help ESL Students Become Fluent and Accurate Readers." *Reading Improvement* 38 (2): 50–61.

Lyons, C. A. 2003. *Teaching Struggling Readers: How to Use Brain-Based Research to Maximize Learning*. Portsmouth, NH: Heinemann.

Macon, J. M., D. Bewell, and M. E. Vogt. 2002. *Responses to Literature*. Newark, DE: International Reading Association.

Marzano, R. 2004. *Building Background Knowledge for Academic Achievement*. Alexandria, VA: ASCD.

———. 2006. *Classroom Practices and Grading That Work*. Alexandria, VA: Association for Supervision and Curriculum Development.

Mathes, P., C. Denton, J. Fletcher, J. Anthony, D. Francis, and C. Schatschneider. 2005. "The Effects of Theoretically Different Instruction and Student Characteristics on the Skills of Struggling Readers." *Reading Research Quarterly* 40 (2): 148–82.

McBride-Chang, C., F. R. Manis, M. S. Seidenberg, R. G. Custodio, and L. M. Doi. 1993. "Print Exposure as a Predictor of Word Reading and Reading Comprehension in Disabled and Nondisabled Readers." *Journal of Educational Psychology* 85: 230–38.

McGill-Franzen, A., and R. Allington. 1990. "Comprehension and Coherence: Neglected Elements of Literacy Instruction in Remedial and Resource Room Services." *Journal of Reading, Writing, and Learning Disabilities* 6 (2): 149–82.

———. 2008. "Got Books?" *Educational Leadership* 65 (7): 20–23.

McGregor, T. 2007. *Comprehension Connections*. Portsmouth, NH: Heinemann.

McKeown, M. G., I. L. Beck, and M. J. Worthy. 1993. "Grappling with Text Ideas: Questioning the Author." *The Reading Teacher* 46 (7): 560–66.

Miller, D. 2008. *Teaching with Intention*. Portland, ME: Stenhouse.

Morrow, L. M., L. B. Gambrell, and M. Pressley, eds. 2003. *Best Practices in Literacy Instruction*, 2d ed. New York: Guilford Press.

Moss, B. 2003. *Exploring the Literature of Fact*. New York: Guilford Press.

National Center for Education Statistics. 1999 and 2009. "The Condition of Education." U.S. Department of Education, Office of Educational Research and Improvement, NCES.

O'Connor, R. E., K. Bell, K. Harty, L. Larkin, S. Sackor, and N. Zigmond. 2002. "Teaching Reading to Poor Readers in the Intermediate Grades: A Comparison of Text Difficulty." *Journal of Educational Psychology* 94 (3): 474–85.

Opitz, M. F., and T. V. Rasinski. 2009. *Good-Bye Round Robin: 25 Effective Oral Reading Strategies*. Portsmouth, NH: Heinemann.

Palinscar, A. S., and D. A. Brown. 1987. "Enhancing Instructional Time Through Attention and Metacognition." *Journal of Learning Disabilities* 20: 66–75.

Paris, S. G., D. R. Cross, and M. Y. Lipson. 1984. "Informed Strategies for Learning : A Program to Improve Children's Reading Awareness and Comprehension." *Journal of Educational Psychology* 76: 1239–52.

Pearson, P. 1999. "A Historically Based Review of Preventing Reading Difficulties in Young Children." *Reading Research Quarterly* 34 (2): 231–46.

Pearson, P. D. 2008. *Teaching Reading Comprehension 24/7*. Presented at Colorado Council Reading Association, February 7.

Pinnell, G. 2006. "Every Child a Reader: What One Teacher Can Do." *The Reading Teacher* 60 (1): 78–83.

Pinnell, G. S., and I. C. Fountas. 1998. *Word Matters, Teaching Phonics and Spelling in the Reading/Writing Classroom*. Portsmouth, NH: Heinemann.

———. 2009. *When Readers Struggle, Teaching that Works*. Portsmouth, NH: Heinemann.

Pinnell, G. S., J. J. Pikulski, K. Wixson, J. R. Campbell, P. B. Gough, and A. S. Beaty. 1995. *Listening to Children Read Aloud*. Research report No. ED 378550. Washington, DC: National Center for Educational Statistics.

Pressley, M. 2002. *Reading Instruction That Works, The Case for Balanced Teaching*. New York: The Guilford Press.

Pressley, M., I. W. Gaskins, K. Solic, and S. Collins. 2005. *A Portrait of a Benchmark School: How a School Produces High Achievement in Students Who Previously Failed*. East Lansing, MI: Michigan State University Literacy Achievement Research Center.

Pressley, M., I. W. Gaskins, and L. Fingeret. 2006. Chapter 3. In *What Research Has to Say About Fluency Instruction*, edited by A. Farstrup and J. Samuels. Newark, DE: International Reading Association.

Pressley, M., S. Symons, B. Snyder, and T. Cariglia-Bull. 1989. "Strategy Instruction Research Comes of Age." *Learning Disabilities Quarterly* 12: 16–31.

Pressley, M., S. E. Dolezal, L. M. Raphael, L. M. Mohan, A. D. Roehrig, and K. Bogner. 2003. *Motivating Primary-Grade Students*. New York: Guilford.

Raphael, T. E., and K. H. Au. 2005. "QAR: Enhancing Comprehension and Test-Taking Across Grades and Content Areas." *The Reading Teacher* 59 (3): 206–21.

Raphael, T. E., K. Highfield, and K. H. Au. 2001. *QAR Now*. New York: Scholastic.

Rasinski, T. V. 2003. *The Fluent Reader*. New York: Scholastic.

Rea, D., and S. Mercuri. 2006. *Research-Based Strategies for English Language Learners*. Portsmouth, NH: Heinemann.

Richardson, J. 2009. *The Next Step in Guided Reading*. New York: Scholastic.

Roller, C. M. 1996. *Variability Not Disability: Struggling Readers in a Workshop Classroom*. Newark, DE: International Reading Association.

Routman, R. 2002. *Reading Essentials: The Specifics You Need to Teach Reading Well*. Portsmouth, NH: Heinemann.

Sadoski, M., and Paivio, A. 1994. "A Dual Coding View of Imagery and Verbal Processes in Reading Comprehension." In *Theoretical Models and Processes of Reading*, 4th ed., edited by R. B. Ruddell, M. R. Ruddell, and H. Singer, pp. 582–601. Newark, DE: International Reading Association.

Samuels, J. 2002. "Reading Fluency: Its Development and Assessment." In *What Research Has to Say About Reading Instruction*, edited by A. Farstrup and J. Samuels. Newark, DE: International Reading Association.

Scanlon, D., F. Vellutino, S. Small, D. Fanuele, and J. Sweeney. 2005. "Severe Reading Difficulties—Can They Be Prevented? A Comparison of Prevention and Intervention Approaches." *Exceptionality* 13 (4): 209–27.

Schmidt, P. 2005. *Culturally Responsive Instruction: Promoting Literacy in Secondary Content Areas*. NCREL North Central Regional Educational Laboratory.

Schwartz, P. 2006. *From Disability to Possibility: The Power of Inclusive Classrooms*. Portsmouth, NH: Heinemann.

Schwartz, P., and P. Kluth 2007. *You Are Welcome: Differentiating Instruction in the Inclusive Classroom*. Portsmouth, NH: Heinemann.

Serravallo, J. 2010. *Teaching Reading in Small Groups: Differentiated Instruction for Building Strategic, Independent Readers*. Portsmouth, NH: Heinemann.

Short, D. J., and S. Fitzsimmons. 2007. *Double the Work: Challenges and Solutions to Acquiring Language and Academic Literacy for Adolescent English Language Learners*. A report commissioned by the Carnegie Corporation of New York. Washington, DC: Alliance for Excellent Education.

Siegel, M. 1985. "More Than Words: The Generative Power of Transmediation for Learning." *Canadian Journal of Education/Revue Canadienne do L'Education* 20 (4): 455–75.

Smith, M., and J. Wilhelm. 2002. *Reading Don't Fix No Chevys*. Portsmouth, NH: Heinemann.

Snow, C., Chair, RAND Reading Study Group, 2002. *Reading for Understanding; Toward a R&D Program in Reading Comprehension*. Santa Monica, CA: RAND.

Snow, C. E., M. S. Burns, and P. Griffin, eds. 1998. *Preventing Reading Difficulties in Young Children*. Washington, DC: National Academy Press.

Stead, T. 2008. *Good Choice! Supporting Independent Reading and Response, K–6*. Portland, ME: Stenhouse.

Stead, T., and L. Hoyt. 2011a. *Explorations in Nonfiction Writing k, 1, and 2*. Portsmouth, NH: Heinemann.

———. 2011b. *Explorations in Nonfiction Writing grades 3, 4, and 5*. Portsmouth, NH: Heinemann.

Steineke, N. 2010. *Assessment Live*. Portsmouth, NH: Heinemann.

Strickland, K. 2005. *What's After Assessment?* Portsmouth, NH: Heinemann.

Taberski, S. 2011. *Comprehension from the Ground Up: Simplified, Sensible, Instruction for the K–3 Reading Workshop*. Portsmouth, NH: Heinemann.

Taub G. E., K. S. McGrew, and T. Z. Keith. 2007. "Improvement in Interval Time Tracking and Effects on Reading Achievement." *Psychology in the Schools* 44: 849–63.

Taylor, B. M., P. D. Pearson, D. P. Peterson, and M. C. Rodriguez. 2005. "The CIERA School Change Framework: An Evidence-Based Approach to Professional Development and School Reading Improvement." *Reading Research Quarterly* 40 (1): 40–69.

Tomlinson, C. A. 2000.*The Differentiated Classroom: Responding to the Needs of All Learners*. Alexandra, VA: ASCD.

Topping, Keith. 1995. *Paired Reading, Spelling and Writing: The Handbook for Teachers and Parents*. New York: Cassell.

Vacca, R. T., and J. A. Vacca. 2008. *Content Area Reading: Literacy and Learning Across the Curriculum*. New York: Pearson.

Valde, G., and L. Kornetsky. 2002. "Transformative Learning." *NEA Higher Education Advocate* (19) 3: 5–7.

Vaughn, S., R. Gersten, and D. J. Chard. 2000. "The Underlying Message in LD Intervention Research: Findings from Research Syntheses." *Exceptional Children* 67 (1): 99–114.

Vaughn, S., and S. Linan-Thompson. 2003. "What Is Special About Special Education for Students with Learning Disabilities?" *Exceptional Children* 69 (4): 391–409.

———. 2004. *Research-Based Methods of Reading Instruction Grades K–3*. New York: Alexandria, VA: ASCD.

Vellutino, F. R., D. M. Scanlon, E. R. Sipay, S. Small, R. Chen, A. Pratt, and M. B. Denckla. 1996. "Cognitive Profiles of Difficult-to-Remediate and Readily Remediated Poor Readers: Early Intervention as a Vehicle for Distinguishing between Cognitive and Experiential Deficits as Basic Causes of Specific Reading Disability." *Journal of Educational Psychology* 88: 601–38.

Walker, B. 2005. "Thinking Aloud: Struggling Readers Often Require More Than a Model." *The Reader Teacher* 58 (7): 688–92.

Walmsley, S. A. 2006. "Getting the Big Idea: A Neglected Goal for Reading Comprehension." *The Reading Teacher* 60 (3): 281–85.

White, T., and J. Kim. 2008. "Teacher and Parent Scaffolding of Voluntary Summer Reading." *The Reading Teacher* 62 (2): 116–25.

Wilde, S., ed. 1996. *Selected Writings of Yetta M. Goodman*. Portsmouth, NH: Heinemann.

Wilhelm, J. 1997. *You Gotta BE the Book*. New York, NY: Teachers College Press.

Willis, J. 2007. *Brain-Friendly Strategies for the Inclusion Classroom*. Alexandria, VA: ASCD.

Wilson, P. T., and R. C. Anderson. 1986. "What They Don't Know Will Hurt Them: The Role of Prior Knowledge in Comprehension." In *Reading Comprehension: From Research to Practice*, edited by J. Oransanu, pp. 31–48. Hillsdale, NJ: Lawrence Erlbaum.

Zambo, D., and W. Brozo. 2009. *Bright Beginnings for Boys: Engaging Young Boys in Active Literacy*. Newark, DE: International Reading Association.

Zemelman, S., H. Daniels, and A. Hyde. 2012. *Best Practice, Fourth Edition: Today's Standards for Teaching and Learning in America's Schools*. Portsmouth, NH: Heinemann.

Index

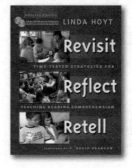